FINDING
HOPE
IN TIMES OF UNCERTAINTY

FINDING HOPE
IN TIMES OF UNCERTAINTY

A Guide to Thriving in the
Challenging World of Today

Joe Bakhmoutski

Finding Hope in Times of Uncertainty: A Guide to Thriving in the Challenging World of Today

Copyright © 2021 Joe Bakhmoutski

All rights reserved. No part of this publication may be reproduced, distributed, or transmitted in any form or by any means, including photocopying, recording, or other electronic or mechanical methods, without the prior written permission of the publisher, except in the case of brief quotations embodied in critical reviews and certain other noncommercial uses permitted by copyright law.

POWER
TO BE HAPPY

PowerToBeHappy.com

ISBN   978-0-6485995-2-4 (print)
       978-0-6485995-3-1 (ebook)

Editor: Ine Baerdemaeker
Cover design: Boris Sabranovic
Interior design: Adina Cucicov

First Edition

Disclaimer: This book is not intended as a substitute for the medical advice of physicians.

Please note: Some names in this book have been changed to preserve the privacy of individuals.

To Olya, for giving me hope

CONTENTS

Introduction: Why Hope Works Now ix

PART 1
THE FIRST CIRCLE OF HOPE: FINDING HOPE

Chapter 1 When Times Are Hard 3
Chapter 2 Safe From Fear 9
Chapter 3 Break Down Confusion 15
Chapter 4 Sail Past Panic 23
Chapter 5 Away From Despair 29
Chapter 6 Make Hope Happen 37

PART 2
THE SECOND CIRCLE OF HOPE: BUILDING HOPE

Chapter 7   From Purpose to Belonging 47
Chapter 8   Confidence Credit 53
Chapter 9   Action As Necessity 59
Chapter 10 The Charge of Resilience 65
Chapter 11 Building Up Hope for the Life You Want 75

PART 3
THE THIRD CIRCLE OF HOPE: SHARING HOPE

Chapter 12 Force of Character 83
Chapter 13 Holding On to Responsibility 89
Chapter 14 Path to Change 97
Chapter 15 Leading With Hope 105
Chapter 16 Sharing Your Hope for a Better Future 119

Conclusion 125
Outro: Accepting Happiness 133
Get in Touch 139
Acknowledgements 141

INTRODUCTION: WHY HOPE WORKS NOW

I first found out about the virus from my oncologist. He rushed in from the airport that morning for our regular check-up. Relieved that I was still cancer free, I asked David about the trip. In a hushed tone, he described the panic at the airport, the rate of replication, and what that might mean for all of us.

In a matter of days, the virus took hold of our world. Infections spiked, and people were dying. The supermarket shelves were swiped clean. It did not completely sink in until a bright yellow and black sign went up for the testing clinic. I turned off the news when I saw the mass graves in New York.

The pandemic is reshaping our world, and governments are scrambling to manage the fallout. But where we need to contain it the most is in our hearts, minds, and souls.

There is a lot of talk about self-care and wellbeing, but many of the standard tools are not made for the times we live in, times of fear and uncertainty. Those tips and tricks can make your life better, but they won't guide you through hardship. As a cancer survivor, I was already aware of this. I knew that we need to look deeper in order to get through the tough times, and build a better life beyond the struggle.

As the gravity of the situation dawned on me, I started looking for ways to keep my worries in check so I could do my work and look after my family. During that search, I was reminded of my grandma's stories about the typhus epidemic of the early twentieth century.

As a 19-year-old medical student in the Soviet Union, she was rushed to a remote mountain village to care for the sick, without any guidance, support, or medical supplies. Quarantine measures were introduced by the state. An armed patrol was ordered to shoot on sight anyone trying to leave the village. Food was in short supply, and nobody knew how long the sickness would last, but people were united by one thing—hope. Hope that things would get better, hope that change would come. Hope became the catalyst that helped people live through the dark times.

We need to adopt that same hope today. Not as a fleeting feeling or a relic of the days gone by, but as an attitude that we take on for life. Beyond the pandemic, we will never become immune to uncertainty. For this reason, we turn to hope for support in overcoming the challenges of life. We look to build hope that guides us towards our goals and helps us fulfil our ambition. Above all, hope is what we share with others in a time of uncertainty and change—it's the true essence of leadership.

Now might be a time when you are struggling to get by. Since you picked up this book, I assume you want to find hope to keep your head above water. Realizing you need help getting through a crisis is the first step of tackling that crisis head-on.

And once you have moved past the worst of it, you might find yourself in an open space where you can look up towards the goals and the ambitions you have, and build up hope to stay the course despite the challenges that will inevitably cross your path. When you have enough hope for the life you want, you will be ready to share it with those who need inspiration and guidance to help them reach new heights in their path to happier, healthier lives.

THE THREE CIRCLES OF HOPE

In this book, I will introduce you to three circles of hope, which are intertwined. Those circles will help you transition from one place in your life to another, on your own terms. Each circle represents one part of the book, and there are transit points between the circles to support life transitions that you might face in your own life.

The first part of the book, *Find Hope*, will help you circle back around to hope in a difficult time. The second part, *Build Hope*, is set up to help you reach your goals and fulfil your ambitions despite the obstacles you will face. In the third and final part, *Share Hope*, we close the circle on hope by sharing it with those who need it the most in times of struggle.

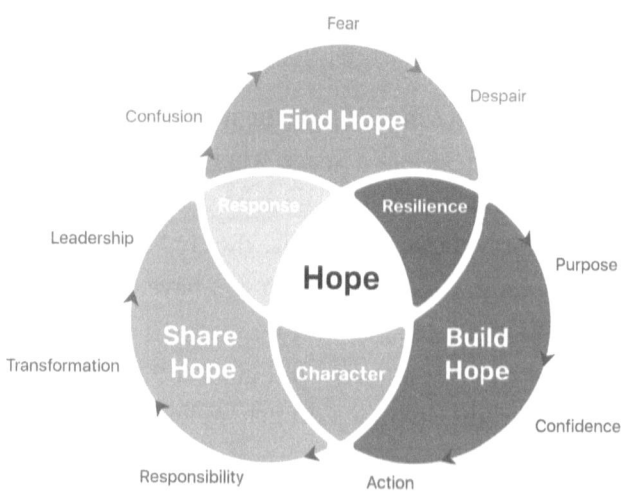

In each part, we go through the core values that we will draw on throughout the journey, along with the tools to get you there faster. I include examples and stories from my life to underscore every point, and exercises will help you build your hope in a way that is consistent with your personal circumstances and your way of life.

In our model, the first circle of hope begins in a place of struggle. Often, our first response leads to confusion, and we are forced to confront fear, panic, and make our way through despair towards hope.

The second circle leads on with hope to reconnect you with your sense of purpose, and to help you borrow the confidence you need to take action towards your life goals and ambitions. Taking action and learning from the inevitable obstacles that rise in your way will help you generate resilience.

The third circle of hope begins with character, which is the foundation for you to accept responsibility for the change you want to see in the world. It will guide you to be the leader that others look to for hope.

This book will help you find hope inside a crisis, have a greater impact on the world when you are facing uncertainty, and help those around you to carry on when times are tough.

Hope is what brings us together. We suffer on our own, but together... Together, we hope!

Part 1

THE FIRST CIRCLE OF HOPE
FINDING HOPE

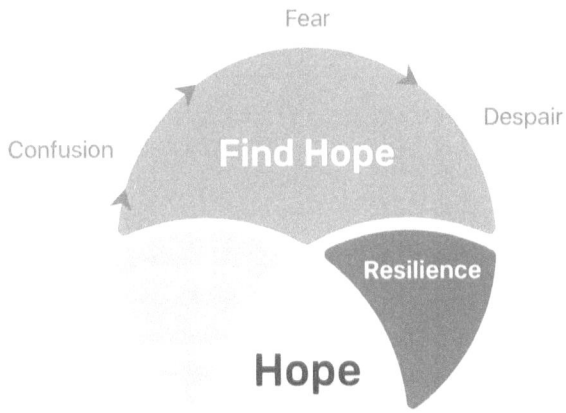

Chapter 1

WHEN TIMES ARE HARD

There are moments in life when you get thrown so far off course that you don't even question what is happening, or why, but go along with the situation because you still can't believe it's real. You know you're in trouble when nothing makes sense, and despite that awful sinking feeling, you still hold out hope that it's all one giant mistake, some kind of cosmic misunderstanding, and it will go away once the people involved realise they have got it all wrong.

But there was no getting away from it, my urologist explained. Scans in hand, he pointed out the exact path that my cancer had taken to get from the testicle into the lymph nodes. Metastatic was my new word of the day.

"This is not good news", he said. "It's in the lymph nodes in your abdominal, and we are going to have to start chemotherapy as soon as possible." I kept nodding my head in response, even though it hadn't got through to me yet.

That morning, I had walked in with the confident stride of a man who expects good news. A quick but necessary formality, nothing more. But why? On reflection, I couldn't find a reason for my optimism. When you believe what you want to believe in, then you must be ready to live with the consequences.

But why was this happening, why me? I'd been a good person, trying to do what's right. I didn't deserve cancer, and how on earth would I stop it from taking over our lives? Why this, why now, when everything had fallen into place—I had finally found the woman I love, and our son was so young.

If the operation had not removed the cancer, then how I could be sure the chemo would work? And if the cancer took over, did that mean I was going to die? But I hadn't accomplished my life's goal... I could not even describe what it was that I have always wanted, I just knew I hadn't done it yet!

Did any of it matter? My thoughts, feelings, gone, like they had never existed. Words turned into a drone, and faded out with the lashing rain as I was trying to process the urologist's words after leaving his office. I had every right to be angry, at myself and the injustice of it all, but all I could feel inside was emptiness.

Later that day, I went to the ocean. There was a raging storm on the water. Massive waves, pounding against the rocks. One after another, they made their way to the shore. Closer and closer, they were searching for a way in. The rocks were strong, but they wouldn't hold out forever. The waves would have their victory, grinding the solid rock into grain, but not today. In another lifetime, maybe, when we are gone.

I was overcome with the enormity of the world around me. This vast space, full of complex systems that have no interest or care for our rules, our circumstances, and the definition of time itself.

The enormity of life is humbling, and, in a way, it releases you from your troubles. It provides you with the freedom to accept the world as it is, and in turn, accept yourself as you are, an integral part of something greater.

This world of ours is not bound by expectations or habit, and neither are you. You are free to do as you like. If you accept things the way they are, then you must also accept that you are not responsible for things you cannot influence, or control.

As for my cancer coming back: If I can't accept what I imagined to be true, then I must accept the thing that turned out to be real.

EXERCISE: ACCEPTANCE

Finding calm begins in the place that speaks to your true nature—the ocean, the mountains, the path near the railway tracks… Most of all, choose a place that speaks to you. A place nearby, where you can be on your own.

Being on your own takes getting used to, but it can set you free! Free to be yourself because you accept that you are only one part of this world. You don't need to fall in line, or be a certain way. No expectations. No pressure.

This becomes a safe place where you can be alone with your thoughts. These thoughts might leak through the gaps and overtake you, but don't be afraid to let them come. This is their domain, to exist, prod, and inspire, but they can't push you around, or pit you against your values and beliefs.

Make it a regular getaway—once a week, or once a fortnight, whenever you need to recover, or find yourself again.

Why not make a plan to do it today or tomorrow?

When you accept things the way they are, you accept the world. You accept that it's here, and so are you. Acceptance puts you on the path to hope.

Chapter 2

SAFE FROM FEAR

What was unusual about that night is that I was home alone. The house was quiet, and I was finishing the day with a long shower.

Funny the way you scrub yourself clean—there is a certain order in which you do things, which is always the same. But when my hand reached down below the waist, there was something foreign, something that did not belong. What was that?! I tried to find it again, and there it was—a big, hard lump on my testicle.

A cold shudder went right through me. It all made sense now—why for weeks, I could not get to sleep due to a dull, burning ache in my groin, and why my underwear felt like it had just shrunk three sizes…

The look of horror on my face must have resembled that of the unfortunate crew member from the movie *Alien*. It's the moment you realise there is a monster inside you, and it's going to burst out and break through the ribcage, and yet, you feel completely powerless to do anything about it.

And now, you can't stop thinking about it. Is it cancer? How long has it been there? Is there any way to get it out? The worry is always there, at the back of your mind.

THE TIGHT GRIP OF FEAR

Your fear, it wants you to leave it alone. To roam free, unchallenged. It will throw you off, close off, distract you, do all it can to prevent you from seeing it up close. Because when you see fear for what it is, you can break the power it has over you.

EXERCISE: UNDERSTANDING YOUR FEAR

To be safe from fear, you have to go to the source of its power. Find the motive—is there a trigger, something that sets you off? Use reason, and not emotion, to guide you. Like a detective investigating a crime, you survey the scene. You examine the evidence to uncover the truth.

Ask yourself:

What am I worried about the most right now, and why?

....

What can I do to prevent this fear from coming true, or to minimise the impact it can have on me, and the people I care about, if it is true?

....

Not long before COVID-19 got its name, I started following the spread of the virus. And I couldn't stop. Watching the number of infections spiraling up, and seeing the reports of more and more people dying from it each day, I felt my heart pounding inside my chest. My mind was racing from one nerve-racking thought to the next. I was wandering around the house like I was lost. I couldn't make sense of my work, or what my son was trying to tell me.

Something had to change. I had to bring order back into my life. I quickly did my Line of Control, the exercise I do to clarify how things stand.

CONTROLLING YOUR WORRY

This exercise helps us separate worries we can't control from the challenges we can manage. Imagine there is a line pointing out from your forehead that divides the space ahead of you in two equal halves. Think of all the worries that seem outside of your control—in the case of the pandemic, this could be the spread of the disease, what the authorities are doing, whether people keep their distance when you are outside, etc. This can help you to manage your expectations because you won't rely on things beyond your control.

From then on, turn your gaze to the right. This is where you put everything that you can change, or at least influence in some way—in the case of the pandemic, you can wear a mask when you go out for groceries, you can change how you interact with friends and family, and you can work from home. This can help you understand where to direct your effort.

From then on, you can pick out the biggest worries that you can influence in some way. Write down what you can do to decrease the chance of them coming true.

When I did this exercise to wrap my head around the pandemic, the three worries that came to mind were:

1. *What if my wife or kids get sick?* I will call our family doctor to organise the tests, and at the first sign of trouble, I will call for an ambulance.

2. *What if we run out of food?* I will stock up on enough food for a month in case we can't leave the house or the shops have to close.

3. *What if I get the virus?* I will pack a bag with spare clothes to stay in the garage, and I will stay there to protect my family from infection until I get better.

EXERCISE: LINE OF CONTROL

Writing your plan out on paper or on your phone gives you a sense of purpose because you are in control of your life.

When you cross paths with worry, what are the top three scenarios you want to avoid?

1. *The first situation I need to be mindful of is…*
   To prevent it from happening or decrease its impact if it does happen, I will…

....

2. *The second situation I need to be mindful of is…*
   To prevent it from happening or decrease its impact if it does happen, I will…

....

3. *The third situation I need to be mindful of is…*
   To prevent it from happening or decrease its impact if it does happen, I will…

....

When you understand your worry, you become fearless—seeing right through it makes you fear less. This way, you are safe from living in fear.

Chapter 3

BREAK DOWN CONFUSION

When you are worried and anxious, you get caught up in thoughts and feelings you did not expect or ask for. To make things worse, your worries get tangled up with events beyond your control, or painful memories that sneak up on you. It can be hard to wrap your head around it.

MAPPING POTENTIAL OUTCOMES

I had to wait for my test results after chemo to find out whether the treatment had worked for six long weeks. No matter what I was doing, whether I was chatting with a friend, having a shower, or eating my dinner, I could not stop thinking:

What if the cancer is still there, slowly growing, taking over my body?

That thought was always there, at the back of my mind. I had to get those worries out of my head, so I took a pen and paper, and on the middle of the page I wrote down "scan result"—there! Now, what was likely to happen from that point on?

I put the two likely outcomes on the page—either the cancer was gone, or it was still there. How likely was it for the cancer to be gone? The treatment works in at least eighty percent of the cases, so that is what I committed to paper. The remaining twenty percent said the cancer could still be there.

Now that it was out of my head, I could look at it in a calmer, more rational way. Those were the odds I was up against, and there was no room for uncertainty to keep plotting against me.

In the worst-case scenario, the cancer was still there. What would happen then? It was such an obvious and simple question, but it's the one I had been afraid to ask, as if saying it out loud would make it more likely to come true. But having come face to face with my fear, I had to see where life could take me.

Having emailed my oncologist, I discovered what we could do if things didn't go plan—an operation to remove lymph nodes, a promising clinical trial, more chemo... Nothing that you would look forward to, but it gave me comfort knowing that another cancer diagnosis would not be the end. This newfound understanding restored a measure of calm back into my life.

I dubbed the overview of possibilities my Outcome Map and carried it with me everywhere—on my nightly walk, on the way to work, when doing groceries. Whenever the worry reared its ugly head, I would dig it out and ground myself in the reality that left little room for misunderstanding, confusion, and overwhelm. This is what my Outcome Map looked like:

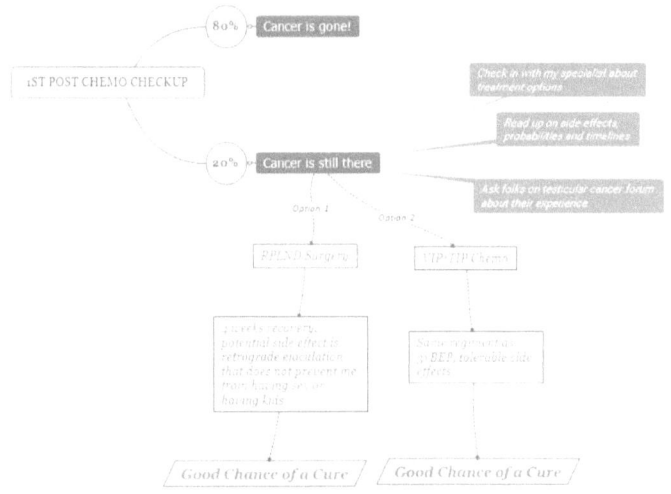

I used the same method when I felt pain in my remaining testicle, and my mind immediately went to cancer: Is it back? Will they have to cut out the testicle, again? I can't lose the last one—my body will stop producing testosterone, and that means no energy, no sex...

These thoughts were driving me crazy, and I had to make sense of what was going on. Armed with a pen and paper, I sat down to write.

I asked myself, what is bothering me the most right now? The pain in my remaining testicle, so that went onto the middle of the page. Next, I wrote out the possible causes and assigned a percentage of likelihood for each cause. This was my best guess based on what I knew at the time.

Here is an example for a specific ache, pain, or worry:

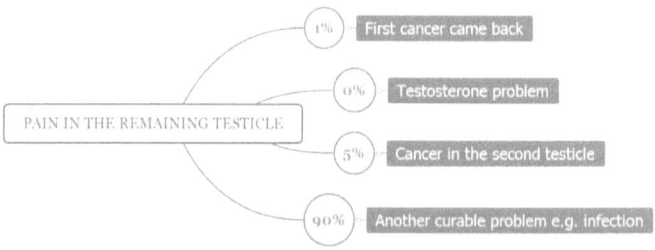

This overview allowed me to look at the situation in front of me and weigh down my options without my emotions getting in the way. This helped me to get on top of worry and inspired me to reach out to my specialist for advice.ç

EXERCISE: OUTCOME MAP

When you are going through a difficult time in your life, it can be hard to make sense of what is going around you. You ask yourself: why is this happening? Am I on the right track? And what should I do now?

You need to find a way past confusion so that you can see the situation for what it is and make rational decisions about what you will do next.

Make your own outcome map. It enables you to visualise all the possibilities of a situation so you can decide what to do next.

You will only need a pen, paper, and five minutes.

In the middle of the page, write down the specific pain, ache, or worry that's troubling you right now. Next, write down each probable outcome.

Outcomes could be a side effect that you read about, a complication from treatment, a muscle problem, or something else entirely.

When you have all the possibilities in front of you, spend 30 seconds on each one to estimate how likely each outcome really is.

It doesn't have to be perfect—we just want to have all the likely scenarios written out to see.

Now that it's all laid out in front of you, it's time to decide what your best course of action is.

What is the one thing you can do about it today?

This approach of getting worries out of your head can help you assess the situation in a calm, rational way so you can decide what to do about it. Here are some prompts to guide you when you want to work through the turmoil you might be experiencing today.

What worries me the most right now is:

....

The probable causes or outcomes are likely to be (short description and percentage):

....

If there is one thing I can do about this today, it is:

....

Break Down Confusion

In times of uncertainty, we cannot avoid bumping into worry, confusion, and panic. They sneak up on you when you least expect it, but when you get your worries out of your head, they lose their grip on you!

Chapter 4

SAIL PAST PANIC

When you are sailing the stormy seas of uncertainty, fear can sweep in without warning. It takes over, trying to undo all the hard work you have so carefully put into place to keep balance, and carry on. One day, I got a glimpse of that sweeping power, and a way to get past it, on the ocean side of Phillip Island, Australia.

As far as the eye could see, the beach was mine, and mine alone. A few kids were playing about, and a girl was walking around with an absurdly large dog beside her, but no one stood between me and the deep, dark blue.

I waded through the water, sending tiny ripples back out to sea. The ocean cold prickled my skin, and soon, I couldn't hold off any longer. I plunged forward, pulling the waters apart with every stroke. A tingle of warmth spread through my body, and I came back to the surface, stretching out onto my back.

The waves were gently rocking me, maintaining a slow, steady rhythm. The deep, dark blue of the ocean was staring back at me from above, and a glint of sunshine was trying to break through the thick clouds.

Unexpectedly, the sky turned to lead, and there was a surge coming from the depths of the ocean below, pulling me back out to sea. I couldn't stand, and the waves tried to swallow me whole. Head back, now! I threw myself back towards the shore, but I couldn't get closer. I was drifting out further, arms flailing, throwing myself against the force that was hell-bent on holding me back.

Suddenly, the waves started picking up, and one hit me right across the face. Smack! There was another one, and another, and one more. Mouth choking with seawater, I splattered out—"Help! Help, somebody help me!" The shore drifted out like a dream. The world went blurry when, as if by magic, a surfer came up over the wave. He helped me onto his board, guiding me back to the shore.

Out of the water, and onto the wet sand, I struggled to get my breath back. "Look, it's the rip that got you," he said. "It's the underwater current. Don't ever try to fight it because it's stronger, and it won't ever let you get back. Don't fight it, just go with it, go sideways and use the rip to get to the shore."

This terrifying experience gave me a new way of looking at panic and fear. When powerful emotions sweep in, it's often easier to let them pass, ride out the charge, and use a brief moment of calm to take back control.

When panic strikes, it comes on suddenly, like a wave that swells up and covers you whole. You are frantic, helpless, not sure what to do. It gets harder when you want to keep your cool so that other people can't see how you are boiling on the inside. To get through the worry storm, look for a place where you can be on your own. Whether you are in a work meeting, or at a friend's house, you might want to excuse yourself, and step out to find a quiet place.

Don't try to control the fear and stop it from happening— doing so saps you of precious energy and might make it swell up even more. The worry is like the storm, raging out at sea. You have your feet planted firmly in the sand, and waves are coming at you, one after another. You don't fight the waves or push them away. Hold your ground and let them come at you. These waves will throw themselves at you, one after another, and yet, you stand firm and let them pass. Breathe in and out, slowly, until there is a calm, steady breath. Breathe, and let it happen.

Once the storm settles, you will feel calmer, but your body will be filled with a frenetic energy that needs a release. Whenever I find myself in that situation, I do a quick, rapid movement to break the tension. With three rapid simultaneous jumps and claps, I snap back to something resembling my usual self. You want to find what works for you—it might be ten push-ups or stomping your feet, as long as it gives you that quick burst of energy, something you can do quickly and anywhere.

EXERCISE: RIDING THE WAVE OF PANIC

When you need to get past panic, try this:

1. Find a quiet space where you can be on your own.
2. Envision your worries as waves that sweep in only to wash past you.
3. Take deep, slow breaths until your breathing is steady.
4. Release the physical tension with rapid body movements.

What are the quiet spots around your home that you might go to when you feel overwhelmed?

....

What is the one thing you can do to get your body moving anytime, anywhere?

....

Fighting fear is a losing game, and trying to control it only makes it last longer. When panic finds a way in, it's best to let it happen and use that momentum to move on with your life.

Chapter 5

AWAY FROM DESPAIR

When you're in a dark place, it can be hard to find the way out. Most people don't see the burden you carry, so it's no wonder there are times when you feel alone. They go on with their lives, and you are stranded with yours. It can be hard to lift your head up when you are struggling to get through the day, and it's easy to take the wrong turn when you have some hard choices to make.

This chapter is about the importance of allowing others to help you in a difficult moment. This might be the time to accept that you should never go through it alone. To accept help from others, and to seek their support is never easy, but we were never meant to brace the perils of life alone!

Just as you stand alongside your partner, your friend, or your workmate when they are having it tough, you can also find the strength to accept their support in turn.

People who care about you will be relieved when you give them an opportunity to step up and be there for you in a meaningful way. There is nothing worse than seeing a friend or a loved one in trouble, and feeling useless, unable to help or create a change in any way.

WITH A LITTLE HELP OF YOUR FRIENDS

Any decision can change your life or the lives of people you care about, in a significant way. Your decisions cannot be undone, so when you are in a tough spot, you might want to set important decisions aside for a time, or check in with someone you trust to make sure your reasons behind the decision are solid and precise.

When you explain the situation out loud, you will have a different understanding of what is going on. You will put your thoughts in words, which often gives you a new perspective and greater clarity on what you want to do next.

Before you take an important decision, find three or more people you trust and describe the situation to them, weighing up the pros and cons of the choice that you are about to make:

"If you have a few minutes, I just want to run something past you. We have a trip overseas coming up, but with the virus, I don't think this would be safe for me and the family. At the same time, I am meant to be the best man at my cousin's wedding, and we have made plans to spend time with the family. But I could never forgive myself if something was to go wrong, so I'm leaning towards cancelling the trip. Does that make sense to you? What would you do differently, and why?"

Even if you are not planning to follow their advice, it helps to get an outside opinion. This way, you are not making a rash decision—there is no hesitation, no misunderstanding, and no regret.

Your loved ones, your friends, and those who truly care about you want to help, but they don't know how! You make it easy for them to be there for you when you explain how they can help you today, or send an email out with a list of practical things they can help you with, and ask people to raise their hand—this way, you are not putting any pressure on them, and giving everyone a fair go at choosing what they would like to help you with.

FINDING SUPPORT IN OTHER PLACES

You will never be a burden to those who care about you, but if that worry is what prevents you from getting the support you need, then the help has to come from outside.

For me, it was the testicular cancer forum. This community, like most, has sprung up to help those in need, united by a shared struggle. They know how you feel, and no one expects you to be a certain way—you can ask questions without being judged, and the people are helpful because they've gone through the same experience.

With people who don't take part in your daily life, there can be no grudges, rivalries, or conflicts to resolve. They don't know you, and there are boundaries they don't need to cross. Share what you will, or don't; it's up to you!

And what a relief it can be to talk to someone who knows how to listen, whether that person is your doctor, a psychologist, or a counsellor. They are not there to judge you or lead you by force; they just want to help. If you don't like their advice, you don't have to go along with what they suggest.

BE THE CHANGE YOU WANT TO SEE

It can be hard to accept help from others, even if there is a part of you that wants you to do just that. There is pride and a sense of independence that you will never want to compromise.

Here's a trick I have taught myself to apply when necessary. It is easier to accept help from those around you when you start giving first. To people who are already a part of your life. To your community. To people that have gone through your struggle. Help can take the shape of a kind word, a smile, or a brief moment that you share with someone, but it can go a long way in times of uncertainty.

What can you do to make a difference to the people you care about the most? How can you make life more meaningful and exciting without giving up on your relationships or compromising your health?

Ideally, it should not take up too much of your time, and fit into your regular schedule—volunteering for one day a month in your community, giving an hourly wage to a good cause every week, or spending one hour a day on a personal project that is not only going to help others, but will also make your life more meaningful, more fulfilling, and more fun.

Giving can be a sign of appreciation and caring. When people do nice things for you on a whim or show their appreciation for what you do, you get a sense of belonging, of being one with the world. Gratitude can even take you by surprise because we don't expect to be acknowledged or celebrated.

How often do you get an email from someone thanking you in a way that does not feel forced, or like it's done out of habit? How often do you get a text with a genuine show of love and care, without the sender expecting anything in return? How often do you get a phone call from someone whose sole intent is to thank you for what you do in the world?

Make no mistake, bringing a smile to somebody's face is a superpower. Making somebody happy, even for a moment, is an accomplishment. This is not to be taken lightly—these simple actions are making your world a better place.

When you cheer people on and help those in trouble, you will find it easier to accept the support that you want for yourself. This will help you understand that you are not alone in this world, and that we all need a helping hand!

A PLACE OF BELONGING

When you lose hope, you need a place to belong. It may seem distant or out of reach, but you will recognise it at once, like an old friend that you have not seen in years. It will explain away the struggle and stop time from sailing past like a dream.

From the time I stood outside the urologist's office in the beating rain, tightly holding on to the pieces of grainy film containing the evidence of the cancer inside me, to the journey through the punishing chemo treatment, and the never-ending wait for results, to the guilt I felt dragging my wife through the fertility process... On my youngest son's birthday, it became clear to me that the moments of pure joy and happiness can only exist because of the preceding struggles.

On that day, Max and I were running loops around our back yard. He was holding on to the tips of my fingers, leading me through the lush long grass towards the bright orange ball. Kick! And then we chased it again, round and round, past the tomato bush, and the lemon tree, and the river gum... Max was babbling with excitement, this world was new, and all I could feel was the warmth of the sun, this bond that we share, father and son, and the charge of being alive.

Having come full circle, I can now appreciate the totality of the experience, with its private joys, the humiliation, and the crossroads. Today, I can see past the hurts, I can look beyond the plans for things that were never going to happen anyway, and the stupid mistakes that I want to forget. And the pain, the pain so real it is almost erased from memory.

I can see life as one, united across time, distance, and the people you meet. It means you don't want to run away from the now, and the future is a treasure map that you carry around with you.

But first, you need to get through the dark times you are facing today. Keep showing up, do enough to survive, and keep moving, at your work, with your family, with your studies, in your community. You may not see hope in the darkness around you, but that does not mean it's not there. I was reminded of that by my one-year-old son who kept pointing at the lights even when they were off. "Light, light," he would cry out in excitement—in the middle of the day. It took me a while to understand why he was doing that. Then I realised he points to the light because he knows where it's meant to be.

Hope is the light that you know is there, even when you can't see it. This is the light that can only appear in the darkness when you stay the course of your life. Give help to others. Give as much as you can give so that you are free to accept help yourself.

Chapter 6

MAKE HOPE HAPPEN

Our journey towards hope begins in the place of struggle. When you are confronted with difficult feelings, it can be hard to pull yourself together again. In our first circle of hope, we talked about finding the strength to accept the challenge you are facing, and how separating what you can and cannot control can help you battle fear and overwhelm.

We also talked about how to map out probable outcomes to put aside our emotions and weigh up the situation in a calmer, more rational way. We closed in on hope by seeking support on your own terms to lead you out of despair:

THE FIRST CIRCLE OF HOPE: FINDING HOPE

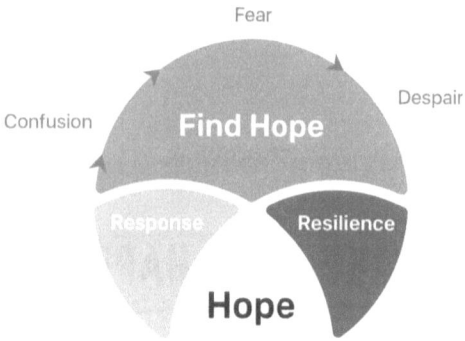

You look to hope to get you through a tough time, but when the struggle is behind you, you can lift the lid on that which is close to your heart. Now, you can dream, and look towards the goals and ambitions in life that you want to achieve.

Maybe what you want the most is to travel the world, or pay off your home, or find a job you don't hate. You might be striving for independence, or being the best parent you can be. But living up to your dreams takes time—there will be distractions and disappointments to throw you off course, so you will need more than motivation to stay on track. That is where hope comes in.

Hope is not loud, or a way to show off. Hope is humbling and does not meddle in the lives of others. Hope is the bridge between wish and expectation for the change that is about to come. When you expect the future to go your way, then you expect great things from yourself because you will be the one to make it happen and to overcome the obstacles that you will inevitably encounter.

SETTING REALISTIC GOALS

If you set the goal to climb the tallest mountain, you will need money for flights, your stay, and the gear. You might want to find a guide, learn a few words in the local language, and figure out the supplies. Those are the challenges you can plan for—you could start putting some money aside each week, so that in a year's time, you can make the trip happen.

You might not want to travel alone. In order to find someone to go with you, you can bring this plan up with people you meet, to see if they are interested, or if they can connect you with someone who shares the passion you have for this journey. You might want to go bushwalking to keep yourself in good shape, start jogging, or find a personal trainer that can help you stay fit.

EXERCISE: REALISTIC GOALS

When you are ready to deal with the obstacles that stand in your way, you set yourself up to win—you are prepared, and there are no surprises.

Use the prompts below to plan for the challenges that are likely to come up.

One realistic goal I have for myself this year is to…

....

The first challenge I expect to stand in my way is…

....

Here is what I can do about it…

....

The second challenge I expect to stand in my way is…

....

Here is what I can do about it…

....

The third challenge I expect to stand in my way is…

....

Here is what I can do about it…

....

Set your own expectations, and you will rise up to meet them. When you can anticipate the challenges that stand in your way, it's easier to find ways around them. This is true for what you want to create in the short and long term.

ACHIEVING LONG-TERM AMBITIONS

If you have the ambition to be a great parent, then you know it won't be easy—you might snap at your child some day and tell them off, and now they are upset. What then? It happens, and I want to be prepared to sit down with my son and say, "I'm sorry I shouted at you. I was busy and tired, but I'll try to do better next time."

What happens when kids don't follow the rules you have set out for them? This is a challenge that parents can expect. It's why you have to find ways to explain the reasoning behind the rules you set, make them easy to follow, and react in a way that shows you are in control of the situation.

As a parent, it can be hard to keep your promises. You make plans, but something urgent comes up, and you need to cancel. How do you explain that to your kids? Will you move the plan to a different time, or change your life around so you can keep your promises?

The choice is yours, but know this—even at your lowest, you are enough. You have enough on the inside to achieve true greatness in a way that is meaningful for you. To be an honorable person, a loving parent, a role model, a true friend.

EXERCISE: YOUR LIFE GOAL

Don't wait for obstacles to ambush you on your way to greatness—use the prompts below to help you prepare:

My one true ambition in life is to…

....

The first challenge I expect to stand in my way is…

....

Here is what I can do about it…

....

The second challenge I expect to stand in my way is…

....

Here is what I can do about it…

....

The third challenge I expect to stand in my way is…

....

Here is what I can do about it…

....

True enough, there will be obstacles on your way to greatness, but having hope will sustain you along your way, and being prepared for life's challenges is a part of making hope happen.

PART 2

THE SECOND CIRCLE OF HOPE
BUILDING HOPE

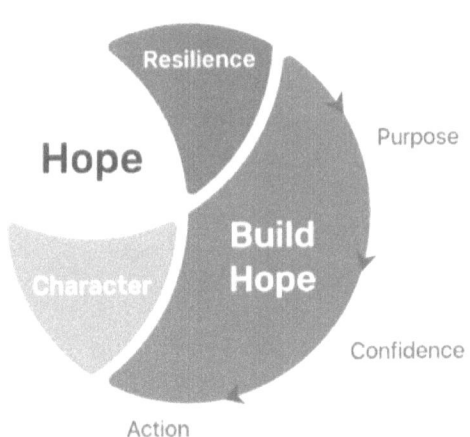

Chapter 7

FROM PURPOSE TO BELONGING

Recently, I was playing in the park with my six-year-old son when his ball rolled off into a ravine. As I went after it, I saw a flock of small birds mobbing a much larger bird. They chased it, beating it down with their wings. The larger bird did not put up a fight or try to get away. Was it hurt? Who was the intruder? I stood there, baffled. And what was my role in all this? Should I stand by, and let nature take its course, or get involved?

Each day, we are reminded that the world around us can be elusive, misleading, and hard to explain. How do you make the right choice in a situation you don't even understand?

Trying to bring order to the chaos around you can be a losing game. Our role, your role, is to restore certainty within yourself. Certainty about who you are, what you believe in, and what you want. This sense of personal conviction can only come from inside—it is ingrained in your beliefs, your values, and how you relate to people around you.

FINDING YOUR PURPOSE

Maybe you find yourself searching for the missing piece of the puzzle that will make your life more deliberate, more grounded, more you. This sense of longing for more is a reminder that your happiness is out there, waiting for you to take it. Don't we all seek to find a greater calling, a purpose that makes our life more rewarding, more meaningful, and more fun?

Having purpose is like warming your hands around a communal fire—you belong to something greater than yourself. This is the reason we are here, in this life, to feel connected, part of a greater whole.

It is the reason we make friends. It's why we fall in love. It's the reason we join clubs, and build cities, and provide shelter in our communities. We want to belong, and our purpose in life is always geared towards helping people that we care about.

And you never get a straight shot at what you want—there is always another random, non-essential task that gets shoved in your face. It pushes to the front of the line, trying to throw you off course or take away the willpower to bring your dreams to life. These tasks might be important, for you and for others, but they must wait their turn—they have their own reasons, and you have yours.

There are times we lose sight of our purpose, and we forget the place and people we belong with. To rediscover your purpose, you want to figure out who you want to help, and why. Finding that person will draw out your reason why you should keep going when you feel like giving up. The person who inspires you may already be a part of your life today—your partner, your child, your best friend, or it might be someone that you gravitate towards based on the shared experience you have, a mutual enemy, or a common goal.

EXERCISE: IDENTIFYING YOUR PURPOSE

These questions can help you clarify your purpose so that you can stay on track towards your dreams despite challenges that will stand in your way.

Who is the person that looks up to me the most right now?

....

Who has lived through a similar struggle that needs help right now?

....

If I could do one thing to help them today, it would be to...

....

How will I know that I am making a difference in a way that is significant to me and my personal values?

....

This is when purpose gets personal—and the underlying reason you have to help those you care about is what compels you to act. You are no longer bound by duty, or deadlines. You are no longer obligated to play by the rules or be seen in a particular way. You are choosing not to get caught up in other people's expectations or plans. Purpose is not only a choice, but the only choice that you make for yourself, over and over, because you want to be free.

And if at times it feels out of reach, that's okay too, because the way you see yourself has been shaped by the past. Those letdowns you may have had are certain to raise doubt about your aspirations and yet, you cannot judge yourself by your setbacks. Aren't we all capable of so much more than we think?

CREATING MEANING

If you know who you want to help and why, you will figure out what you need to do to make it happen. To support my friend during a break-up, I don't start out with a plan—I wonder how he is doing, and I give him a call to ask if we can catch up on the weekend. What you do comes about naturally because you want to make a difference in a way that is consistent with your values and your way of life.

If your reason serves to protect, and never to hurt, and if your purpose is to give, and never to take away, then the purpose is universally valid, by default. When you give your energy to those in your life you care about the most, when you devote your creativity towards meaningful projects that help out your community, when you give a helping hand to those around you who may be struggling right now, when you give time to a cause that speaks to you on a deep, personal level, you can do no wrong!

It may not be easy to start, but you have lived through the struggle, and you have overcome—you are still here, and you have the strength to give your best. You can contribute in a way that is meaningful to you, and is consistent with your values and the way you want to see yourself out in the world.

With purpose, you belong with those you care about the most. You are reaching for goals that never feel forced, and ambitions that no one can take away. Now, you only need the confidence to take the next step.

Chapter 8

CONFIDENCE CREDIT

Revealing yourself to strangers is hard—you don't want to be judged or feel like a failure. So when you are going for a job interview, landing a new client, or going on a first date, you might say to yourself, "I wish I had more confidence to get it right."

These are the things you can't get around doing—you can't fall in love without getting to know the person first. You won't get the job you want when you are not prepared for the interview. You won't get the client if you don't understand their world. We need to bring out the confidence before we can take the necessary steps forward in life.

THE SECOND CIRCLE OF HOPE: BUILDING HOPE

PLANNING FOR HOPE

Confidence starts with having a plan. When you dress up in clothes you feel comfortable in, you are bound to be more relaxed. When you plan to arrive on time for your interview, or your first date, you leave less room for worry. When you know what you want to talk about, you don't have to think on the spot. But even the best preparations can come undone when things don't go to plan. They hardly ever do, and while planning is a start, hope is what keeps you going.

Like a ship bracing the open sea, you expect stormy weather to throw you off course, but you hope for the better—that you will hold on when the going gets rough, that you will find a way forward, that good change will come.

Let's say you are looking to buy your first home. Most people can't buy property outright, so you take out a loan from the bank. You pay the loan off over time, but the home is essentially yours.

With confidence, you borrow it against the hope that things will turn out well. The hope that, when you hit an obstacle, you will find a way around it. When you are at the crossroads, you will find the courage you need to make the best decision you can. When all else fails, you will not give up, and go on in the hope that you will figure out the way forward.

You borrow confidence against hope to stay sane, steady, and strong in the face of uncertainty. But how do you pay back the credit you take out against hope? You repay the confidence with results. Every mistake, every misstep is a result because it's an opportunity to learn what you can do better next time and to recognise progress within the greater view of your own experience.

Results are necessary because they bring you closer towards fulfilling your ambitions and shape the way you see yourself. For example, buying your first home can be a vital part of your independence. Ambition is personal because it speaks to your higher self and pulls you up towards the life you want to lead.

TRIAL AND ERROR

When my first long-term girlfriend left me for another man, my life fell apart. I would go from screaming rage into complete withdrawal in a matter of minutes, and back again. My panic attacks were making it hard for me to go outside or be around people. I drank myself to sleep most nights. I wanted to meet someone, anyone who would lift me out of this misery. I went on one date after another, but nothing was going my way. I wanted to shut in and stop trying.

Still, I wanted to love, and to be loved in return. I wanted to find the right woman, but how? I had no idea how to meet people. Going on dates was daunting, and I had no idea how to tell if she was into me, or if I even liked her at all. My confidence hit rock bottom, and the only way to get it back was to keep going, in the hope that I could figure things out, and that my ambition to find love would find its way. I kept going, using the confidence I borrowed against hope.

I kept trying new things—speed dating, short courses, and dating websites. Most of what I did was wrong, but every little win gave me confidence to keep going. It took three years before I found the woman who makes me feel like I am living on the horizon. On the journey to finding her, there were countless times I questioned myself, losing heart, mind, and soul, but hope kept me going, through the storms and the shipwrecks.

Every mistake, every misstep is a good result when you can learn from it and do better next time. But results are easy to miss, or brush aside, especially when you are building something over time, so I advise you to bring those results to light, to recognise and celebrate what you have achieved as part of what you do each day.

CELEBRATING SMALL WINS

When you think of what you have achieved to reach your goals and your ambitions, when you reflect on what you have achieved in a way that is deeply ingrained in your daily life, when you keep track of your results in your diary, you give yourself the credit you deserve for doing what you can to survive and keep moving.

Those results might not always be grand, but they are necessary steps you take to give yourself a sense of progress, and to convince yourself to keep going in the right direction. These steps are the essence of our life, and we cannot take them as a given. We need to care for them, nurture them, and look upon them with pride, as they prove that we are gaining ground on our dreams and are consistently striving to get better.

EXERCISE: PERSONAL WINS

Aim for one small win each day, and reflect on the accomplishments you have achieved. Here are two prompts to use daily:

Yesterday I accomplished:

. . . .

If there is one thing I do today that I can be proud of, it will be to:

....

Write down anywhere between five and ten results you have achieved. It works best when you keep them simple—whether it's something that helped you grow or that made a difference to someone you care about, be sure to include it in your list. Every moment that fills your life with meaning counts, whether it's working on a new idea, checking in on a friend, or enjoying a quiet dinner alone.

Often, you forget what steps you are taking towards the life you're proud to have, and you blame yourself for not doing enough. Or you don't give yourself enough credit for taking the necessary steps towards your goals. Accepting credit for your accomplishments, no matter how small they seem, can help you build confidence because you know what you have achieved and feel accomplished for what you do in your life each day.

You borrow confidence against hope and repay it with results. Day after day, you are moving closer to reaching your goals and fulfilling your ambitions because no matter what anyone says, you are enough. You have the power to turn things around when you keep track of your progress and give yourself the credit you deserve.

Chapter 9

ACTION AS NECESSITY

I used to feel guilty after dropping our son off at kindergarten. I can't tell you why—my wife and I had to work, so we had a good reason. Still, I couldn't shake the feeling that I was doing something wrong.

On my way out, I would peek through the window to see how he was getting on, and I couldn't help but marvel at the teacher keeping their cool despite the mayhem. How do you stay calm with twenty-five screaming kids around? Each one wants a different toy, or needs to go to the toilet, or wants to go outside to the yard… On top of that, you have to stick to the timetable with the alphabet, story time, and the meals. How on earth do you get anything done?

Our lives are like that—there are many tasks fighting for your attention, and it's hard to find time for that which you care about the most. Even when you have got your eyes on a goal, with purpose to guide you and the confidence to move forward, you still need to stick to the path despite the chaos around you.

You follow your instinct to survive. You don't think; you act. If your house is on fire, flames are licking at the walls, and the smoke is making it hard to see, you won't wonder—should I stay, or should I go? You don't stop to weigh up the options; you make a run for it! You act out of necessity, which is the simplest way to get things done because it requires no decision making on your behalf.

CREATING NECESSITY

When we want our precious, best-guarded dreams to turn true, we must elevate our goals and ambitions to the level of necessity. That way, there is no way to go around them, they take the front seat, no matter what, and you will get things done.

You need two ingredients to create necessity.

The first one is your **net dream**—you want something so badly that you will do whatever it takes to make it come to life! It can force you to set aside your comforts and guilty pleasures. It might take years of frustration and disappointment. It sure won't please everyone, but you will see it through when you have your reason pulling you forward.

This reason might not have formed in your mind just yet, but when you are able to put it into words, and give it a shape and meaning that are unique to you and your way of life, it will guide you towards achieving your goals and ambitions. For it is easier to find the path towards that which you desire when you know exactly what you are looking for. And if your net dream is not a luxury but a necessity, then you go after it with every bit of strength and courage you can muster.

Secondly, you need to face the **consequences of what you stand to lose** if you miss out on your dream. With every goal you aim for, with every ambition you strive for, you are taking a risk. We live in the world of opposites—when there is one thing to be gained, there is always another to be lost. The risk you take in forging ahead with your ambition in life can be a constant cause of concern, or become your source of inspiration moving forward.

So what is on the line for you when you are aiming for happiness? What do you stand to lose if your plans come to nothing?

The first feeling that comes over you might make you anxious, worried, or upset. But this first reaction is only a warning that you need to watch out for danger. Even if you take the wrong turn or get pulled aside, you can find the courage to find your way back on track!

EXERCISE: CREATING NECESSITY

These prompts can help you bring more clarity to the dream you want to make reality.

If there is one thing I will regret not doing, it will be...

....

If I'm honest, what worries me the most about pursuing my dream is...

....

If I miss the chance to make my dream come to life, I'll surely know about it when...

....

HOW CANCER HELPED ME GET FIT

For years, I tried to get fit. I joined the gym, started diets, and forced myself to stay away from snacks. But those good habits never stuck, even though I set new resolutions for myself, year after year. There was no real reason for me to keep going, so I quit trying.

Cancer changed all that. When I got home after my treatment, my son would jump on the bed, screaming: "Papa, let's do a cushion fight!" In the weeks before, I had missed our silly games, when we wrestled and threw toys at each other. But after my treatment I was so weak that I said, "Sorry, my friend, I'm so tired. Let's do this another time." Head down, he left the room.

Fighting back tears, I thought—what sort of a father am I going to be? The thought of missing out on the best days of my life, with my son, feeling useless and sorry for myself, was too much to bear. I needed to figure out how get my life back in order!

I had never jogged in my life, but I figured there was only one way to get started. The first jog barely lasted two hundred meters. My legs got so heavy, they refused to move. I stopped dead in my tracks, gasping for air. Next day wasn't much easier, but I kept going. Week after week, it got easier. I got into a habit and started looking forward to my morning jogs.

Two years later, I can not only chase the ball out on the soccer field with my son, but I also take our new baby for long strolls with the pram every morning. Having the energy to be with my boys is the reason I keep fit. This is a big difference with where I began, and I'm not going back! There is no need to force myself to exercise and eat better because my everyday life has caught up with how I see myself today.

Elevating your goals and ambition towards necessity is the most direct route to getting things done. There is no confusion—the choice is clear, and it compels you to act.

Chapter 10

THE CHARGE OF RESILIENCE

You can regain your grit and composure after going through a challenging time. It isn't the struggle that has made you more resolute, but what you did in order to survive and get through it. Resilience is our ability to adapt in the face of adversity, and to take from our own experience that which can make us stronger.

HARD TIMES, HARD TRUTHS

Looking out of the window of the oncology ward, I saw kids eating ice cream, people in a rush, carrying on with their lives as if nothing was wrong. This would be my year without summer—just this once, if things went to plan.

Next to me in the ward was Simon, a friendly, fun-loving guy my age. Every day, I saw his friends and family come over to visit, and I could not help being jealous. I told my friends where to find me, but it had been a week, and I hadn't heard from them.

Then it came to me—of course, the hospital must be jamming the signal on my phone so that it wouldn't interfere with the medical equipment. My people couldn't get through—why hadn't I thought of that before? To check if my guess is right, I decided to try and call my mobile. I got up from the bed to find a landline.

The ward was shaped like a lifebelt, with a nursing station and supply room in the centre. Slowly, I made the round trip, dragging my drip behind me. I saw the landline on a nurse's desk. There was no harm in trying—it would go straight to voicemail anyway, or not get through at all.

But to my surprise, my mobile phone came to life in an instant. It lit up, like a carnival, playing its silly jingle. I couldn't take my eyes off it, as if in a trance. This was it, I realised. Nobody was coming.

In the weeks that followed, I tried my best to set this newfound knowledge aside. But the memories came surging back when I got a call from a missing friend. I could not bear to hear his voice, so I let it ring and went outside. I shouted curses, in a rage, howling at the night.

How could they leave me alone like this, and disappear, right when I needed them the most? I could not wrap my head around it. Was there something wrong with me so that they didn't want to be around? Or were they being selfish and cruel? I played these thoughts over and over in my head, trying to find answers.

I wasn't alone in my experience. Many cancer survivors I speak to on my podcast *Simplify Cancer* have gone through a similar experience, and here are the three reasons why. The first is that people are afraid of death and dying, and my cancer brought up troubles they did not want to face. The second reason is that no one wants to feel stupid or insensitive. If you want to avoid saying or doing the wrong thing by accident, then sometimes, it's easier to do nothing at all. The third reason is that people can grow apart. It can be hard to notice at times because we are busy with our own lives, and it can take an unexpected twist of events to bring home the reality that the closeness you once had is now gone.

These reasons fit. They explained much about why most of my friends backed away, but that did not make it easier for me to live with it. The crucial point was, how could I make sure this would never happen again? I thought long and hard about what it is I want from my future friends.

Look, I want people to show up in my life because they want to be there, and not just when it happens to be convenient. I want my life's work to be a natural part of the conversation, not a box-ticking exercise. I want friends who pull me up, not drag me down with them.

HOW YOUR VALUES CAN SHAPE YOUR RESILIENCE

Having honed in on my personal values has helped me clear out the reservations I had about meeting new people, and identify the qualities I have to offer as a friend. There is no longer any doubt about what I have to do, and what I am looking for in people. Yes, it takes time and effort to bring these people into my life, but it has also become easier for them to find me.

When you are in line with your internal compass, you have greater clarity about what you can expect from yourself and the world around you. That does not mean you have to lower your standards—no, you raise the bar to where it should have been from the start!

Resilience is not the wall that will keep your world from toppling down, but your ability to match your expectations with your values when the only choices left are to sink or swim. The closer they are aligned, the better prepared you are for the curveballs that life throws your way.

We can only build resilience if we look at life as a series of manageable situations. If the challenge ahead of you feels monumental, then you are likely to be overwhelmed. It will feel like nothing can be done. We want to break down the challenge you have in front of you in such a way that it feels manageable and you can handle it in a reasonable way.

EXERCISE: FIGHTING SMALL BATTLES TO WIN THE WAR

As you get ready to face the day, it can be helpful to pick out a specific problem that you know you are going to face today. It may be part of a bigger struggle, or a difficult task that you want to get out of your way.

You might not have a way to get around it, but giving your struggle a name and identifying your desire to get through it can help you to hang in there and keep going.

Use this prompt in your journal to pinpoint the challenge up ahead:

If there is one challenge I'm ready to face today, it's...

. . . .

Identifying one challenge that you will face each day can give you more clarity about the struggle you have, and a greater degree of control over what is happening in your life because you approach life with the belief that you can handle difficulties that stand in your way.

Often, you are forced to reflect on your values when you are going through a challenging time, but you don't have to wait for adverse circumstances to force your hand. If you make this process a part of your regular life, it will help you find peace with the past you left behind and become more resilient in the face of challenges that life throws your way.

REFLECTING ON PERSONAL VALUES

As part of my morning routine, I go to the garden to think back on the two or three people who helped me grow. I take the time to wonder about what I would miss out on without their presence in my life. Those who gave me their kindness without expecting anything in return. Those who pushed me to go on when all I wanted was to turn back. A few minutes each day is all you need to ground yourself in things that are true to you and your way of life.

When I think of my mum and how she has helped me grow, I find myself in my old fold-out bed in the lounge room. My teddy is propped up against the pillow, and the sunlight is breaking through the curtains. My mum bursts in from the cold of winter, holding a book in her hands: "Look what I got for you!", she says. The book has a peculiar title, and yet there are familiar faces on the cover… It's the sequel we had been hoping to find for months! She is beaming at me, and this day will be the best one of all. This memory speaks to the unconditional love she gave me, and the belief I hold on to in times of struggle that no matter what, I deserve to be loved.

EXERCISE: BRIGHT MEMORIES

What are the brightest memories that you treasure? This can be a quiet moment you shared with your spouse, or a fun time you had with a close friend. These moments bring out the connection you share, and how their influence has helped you become the person you are today.

Can you think of three to four people who have had an impact on you? Here are two questions that may help you bring out those memories:

Who has helped me grow and be the person I am today?

. . . .

What distinct moment with them stands out the most?

....

Bringing this memory to light can take several minutes when you first try it, but over time, the moment will come rushing back to you at the flick of a switch. It's an easy habit to get into when you make it a part of your everyday routine, whether you go for a walk at a certain time, have a shower, or finish your breakfast.

RECOGNISING PAST VICTORIES

To be more resilient, you want to recognise the times when you live through the tough times in the past, and do more of what helped you then. A true victory is not always the climb to the tallest mountain, or defying the odds, but retaining a sense of self in the face of adversity.

EXERCISE: PAST VICTORIES

To bring out the times when you stood your ground, ask yourself:

When was the one time when I came this close to giving up completely, but somehow found the strength to keep going?

....

What helped me then, and how can I use it against the challenges that life throws my way?

....

This is a reminder of how far you have come and what you are capable of. And when you feel like gravity will not hold you, you can anchor yourself in a safe place and stand your ground, or get back up swiftly if you fall.

Chapter 11

BUILDING UP HOPE FOR THE LIFE YOU WANT

Only when I returned home after chemo, did I realise just how much I had missed the simple things—sleeping under a quilt, choosing what food I wanted from the fridge, and going to the toilet with the door closed.

Rejoicing in my newfound abilities, I brewed a strong pot of freshly ground coffee. With a steaming hot cup of java in my right hand and a book in my left, I headed towards our little garden out the back. I had earned the right to enjoy my time back—at least until the results would come back.

Coming out onto the porch, I felt odd, like parts of me were coming apart at the seams. Fatigue from the chemo came on, like a sudden wave, leaving me nauseous and weak. The swing bench I was aiming for is only a stone's throw away from the porch, but every step was excruciating. I thought of my grandfather's colossal effort in reaching the kitchen table—at 86, he was fifty years my senior. Was this the struggle I was going to face each day?

With the journey to the swing bench behind me, I took a good sip of my coffee. Yuck! I nearly spat out the murky, disgusting liquid. Thanks, chemo… Would I ever get my taste buds back?

I put the cup to the side and opened the book. It had arrived at our home when I went to the hospital, and I had been looking forward to it ever since. But now I stared at the words, wondering how they fit. My head started spinning, and I was struggling to keep myself together. I set the book aside and buried the face in my hands.

How was I going to get through this? I couldn't go to work like this! Or play with my son, or be there for my wife… But I couldn't give up. I had worked so hard to build out my life, so I had no choice but to see it through! I had been through worse before and had come out stronger. I could turn things around. I would ask my specialist and our doctor. There had to be a way! If others had gone through it, so could I. I just needed to get through the day...

Allowing myself to dream turned me back towards hope—when you are asking how things can change, you are searching for the way through.

Back on the swing bench, I caught glimpses of people around me. My wife, my son, and complete strangers... They were smiling, talking excitedly, listening with intent. There was something I needed to say, and somehow, I was in the centre of it all, and instinctively, it felt right. These visuals were blending, like a mosaic. It was a coming together of past, present, and many possible futures, joining in to form a life of impact.

I realised that going through cancer did not have to hold me back—I could use my experience to help others who are forced to confront it. In the process, it would make me a better father, a better husband, a better human being. Finding that sense of purpose was the first station on the second circle of hope and it made me feel like I belonged again, because something personal was now at stake.

So where did I begin? I got into podcasts during treatment—it's easy to do when you are resting in bed, and you feel like you're a part of the conversation. I'd never done a podcast before, so I was full of questions—where do I even begin? Do I need special equipment to record? How do I find the right guests, and will they even want to be a part of the show? I'm not a scientist or a doctor—so why would anyone listen to me?

I told myself, even if no one listens, I need to do it for me, first. No daydreams, no shortcuts, no regrets. You stumble forward, and things fall into place, like the stars. That was the second station on the second circle of hope, where I built hope for the impact that I wanted to make. Borrowing confidence against the hope that I had, rather than waiting for it to strike out of the blue one day, gave me the freedom to begin.

I received praise from listeners and experts alike after launching the podcast, which led me to write a book called *Simplify Cancer: Man's Guide to Navigating the Everyday Reality of Cancer*. Finding my purpose and the confidence to move forward got me to the third station of Building Hope, where I had no choice but to make things happen. I would never have dreamt of authoring the *Simplify Cancer* book had I not built up the confidence of doing the podcast. The response I got helped me find my voice, building up the momentum to move forward.

Writing did not come easy. I struggled to get my thoughts out on paper, and when I did, it was to confront the past hurts and mistakes that I made. But I kept at it, forcing the necessary words out of me. Because there is no other way—when you have hope, you will find the strength to carry on. It has helped me to not only find resilience, but to also sustain it and let it grow. With resilience, we have come full circle to a renewed hope that can fuel our sense of purpose, amplify our confidence, and spur us to action!

THE SECOND CIRCLE OF HOPE

This is the journey through the second circle of hope:

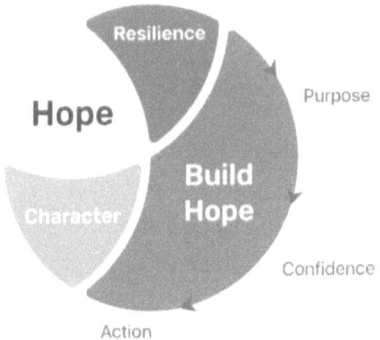

Hope is what leads us out of despair and towards fulfilling our ambitions. It's the journey we go on to rediscover our sense of purpose and find the confidence that helps us to keep going, so that taking the necessary action towards our dreams is but an afterthought. Building hope makes us more resilient to the inevitable challenges that await us in times of uncertainty.

PART 3

THE THIRD CIRCLE OF HOPE
SHARING HOPE

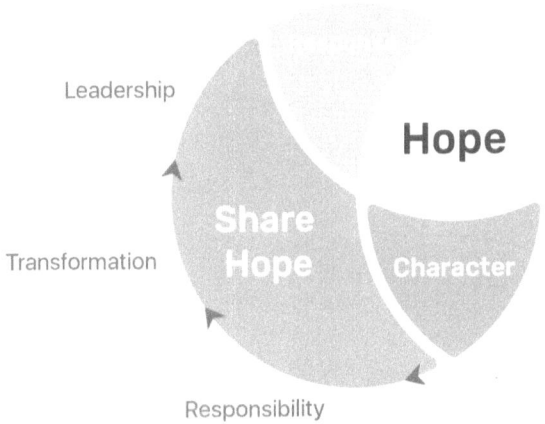

Chapter 12

FORCE OF CHARACTER

How can you give hope to someone who is hanging on by a bare thread? Hope can be hard to put into words, but you feel it, trembling, like the heat coming from a fire.

Hope, like love, cannot come from a place of doubt or hesitation—you go all in because there is no other way. This is the character you forge through life, and it draws people in to take part in your story of hope.

IDENTIFYING CHARACTER

When you have character, people listen to you more. Character adds more weight to the arguments you put forward because people trust that you speak your truth. Character gives you a kind of presence that is inescapable—it seeps through the smallest gestures and leaves a mark for a lifetime. When I think of the person my grandfather was for me, it's the impact he made with the smallest things that stands out to me the most.

Maybe it only happened this once, but when my grandfather came to pick me up from kindergarten, I knew it would be a day to remember. As we made our way to the bus stop, I proudly held his hand.

The driver was wiping off the sweat from his forehead, as my grandfather counted out the change for our tickets. Inside, the bus was bursting with heat. Reluctantly, the passengers gave up on the small talk to stare out of their windows at the listless, sun-bleached world.

My grandfather pointed at the only spare seats, "Look here, boy—best seats in the house! Get in quick, or we'll miss out." He winked at the passengers, "These good people, they might be jealous, but finders keepers, isn't that how it goes?" He let me take the seat by the window.

"You will forgive them, my boy, they are in a rush, just as we are, for the game tonight." His voice, booming like the loudspeaker, "For this biggest match of all, surely, we find eleven players to do our country proud! He turned at the people around us, "That isn't too much to ask for, is it, friends? To be the champions of Europe? This is football, and we're pretty good at that, aren't we?"

As if they'd been waiting for a signal, the passengers surged back to life with a burst of smiles, murmurs, and excitement.

My grandfather leaned in closer to whisper, "We are up against the big boys tonight, my boy, but that is between you and me." He beamed, nudging me with his elbow, "In any case, we'll have a good time, won't we, my boy?"

I nodded excitedly, knowing that no matter what, we were going to win, and that this moment, this life, full of brightness and expectation, was only meant for me, only me.

Character isn't a role we choose to take on, but a reflection of who we are in the hearts and minds of the people around us, in the myriad of private memories and individual impressions.

FOLLOW YOUR CHARACTER TO AVOID REGRETS

You forge your character by leading a regret-free life. A life without doubt or second-guessing yourself. A life with clear-cut decisions and nothing to hide. You will only do that which you believe in, wholly and without reserve.

This is not a pipe dream. Each day, you default to your emotions and logic when you make decisions. You are deeply rooted in who you are today, but when you look at the situation from the vantage point of avoiding regret, you delve into the future where your choices are more in line with your values.

You will never know if the decision you took led you to the exact place where you wanted to end up, but you will be safe in the knowledge that this was the only reasonable choice you could make at the time.

A regret-free life is not about dismissing past wrongs or absolving the guilt you feel. If you can make mistakes, you are entitled to reflect on the decisions that took you down the wrong path. It's how you learn to do better next time and turn your back on regret that belongs to the past!

Every time I talk to my grandmother on the phone, she reminds me, "Being a doctor was fine, but I should have pushed hard with my research and have focussed on getting published."

To this I can counter, "But look at your life, grandma—you healed thousands of people, you have a disease named after you... You can't be this hard on yourself!"

For a moment, the line goes silent.

"If only… I wish I could turn back time. At my age, the only thing you are left with is the past and what you have failed to do."

With sudden conviction, she then says, "Don't ever settle for anything, because it's never enough. You must never lose your hunger, or you will forever wonder what it is exactly that you have missed."

A regret-free life is an extra lens to look at the situation before there is any decision to be made—will I blame myself for not doing this in a year's time? Is this the moment where I let an opportunity pass me by? Is this the choice I will regret not making when I look back on it tomorrow, next year, or when it's too late?

A regret-free life does not make you more dignified or deserving of happiness. Instead, it's a chance for your character to shine and for people to see you the way that you are—in tune with your aspirations and the hope you want to share with others.

It is easier to live with uncertainty when you look back and think—I regret nothing and look forward to everything.

Chapter 13

HOLDING ON TO RESPONSIBILITY

In times of uncertainty, we start doubting ourselves and questioning what we do in the world. We look for support and encouragement, and as a leader you want to help people in need. If leading refers to doing a good thing for those in need, then you are always leading—in your family, with people you work with, in your community. Leading yourself, too, as you are always striving to be a better person. But accepting the responsibility to lead is no easy task, and there are three reasons why.

THE HURDLES

First, there are no guarantees that you will get your way in life. You want to be at your best to uphold your innermost hopes and dreams, and nothing is ever promised. When you cast aside the promise of swift success, you free yourself from false expectations and get closer to the people you care about the most. To get behind you, your people need proof that you are in charge of your hopes and ambitions. For how can they hold you in high regard if you don't accept responsibility for the future you want to be a part of? How can they trust you, when you don't trust yourself to chase after your dreams? Authenticity draws you in, like a sunrise—you have the freedom to speak your mind, stick to your word, and stake your claim about the future you want today!

The second reason we push responsibility away is we don't want to suffer the consequences. We are told to do our part, but doing your part often stands for doing the bare minimum! You don't go halfway when it comes to being a good parent or a loyal friend—no, you give everything you have and hope that it's enough... When what you seek is a real connection, when you want to leave a legacy behind that is going to last, you will bypass the essentials and strive for your absolute best.

Being someone's soul mate, a true supporter, the confidante, these are not half-hearted parts you play! The role itself demands a higher level of responsibility—you commit yourself to caring, cherishing, and supporting. Accepting responsibility means you expect more from yourself. And rightly so, for how could you allow yourself to fail when each new day, you are capable of greatness?

The third reason we give up on responsibility is that we can feel powerless to change things. If you look at life as a series of random events that you have no control over, you become disheartened—because nothing is going your way. You descend into pity, and that is exactly where I found myself after a painful breakup.

THE PROMISE AND THE PAY-OFF

My ex, I blamed her for everything. And not without reason, since she had affairs and left me for another man. I kept unpicking the hurtful things she had said, and the now obvious signs of what went on, and why I was looking the other way. She followed me, like a ghost, and there was no escape from the stupid mistakes I made in trying to change her.

Why and how could anyone do this, I screamed at the traffic lights. There was darkness around me, but one thing I saw clearly, that from now on, I would never let anyone do anything like this to me, ever again.

After that experience, what could I do to prevent this from happening in the future? First, I needed to start believing—

in myself, and that I deserve to be loved, again. I started eating healthy food and keeping fit. I learned how to look other people in the eye, literally—first, by making eye contact with passers-by on the street, then with cashiers at the supermarket, and later with women I wanted to meet.

I started having fun when I was out on a date, and it showed. My confidence grew, and I knew that meeting the woman I wanted to find was only a matter of time. Because no one is responsible for finding the right woman but me.

When you have no fallback plan, where you are not relying on pure luck or chance, you put yourself in situations where the result is inevitable. The more responsibility you keep, the easier it becomes to make a change. The more responsibility you can hold on to, the easier it is to deal with disappointment and stand up to life's challenges on your terms.

But responsibility was the last thing on my mind when I came into the hospital for the first cancer treatment cycle. I looked up at the black drip bag that hung over me like a storm cloud. The clear liquid was snaking its way down the tube and into my vein. There was no escaping it now—I was chained to the life of uncertainty. How sick would it make me? Would it take away the cancer? Or am I going to die?

Holding On to Responsibility

The anguish of seeing my wife and my mom trying to hold it together was tearing at me on the inside. I couldn't fall apart, not at that point—I had to hold it together, for their sake and mine. I had to do everything in my power to handle cancer in such a way that I didn't push my people out any further. I had to put my trust in the process, do everything in my power to let go of things I couldn't control, and hope that it would be enough.

From celebrating our son's third birthday in my cancer ward, to finding sanctuary in the reeds of the hospital garden, we dug deep to find our way through. The struggle was real, but we pulled through—together!

I kept the promise I had made to myself. And yet, there was no one at the finish line, cheering me on for making good on the commitment I had made. No one held me to account, but making it through on my terms was enough.

EXERCISE: YOUR PERSONAL PROMISE

What is the ultimate promise you make to yourself today that is worth keeping?

The promise you make to yourself, and stick to, is the only promise worth keeping. No one might give you the credit for it, or even acknowledge it in any way, but deep down inside, you will live through it, knowing that you stood up for yourself and what you believe in. You don't need to shout it from the rooftops or flaunt your accomplishments in front of others.

A DIFFERENT APPROACH TO LIFE

Accepting responsibility in life makes it easier to stay on track. There is no doubt, no hesitation, and no fear because you know that no one will do it for you. This commitment can be the greatest source of pride and joy when you accept responsibility for the benefit of others.

We take on different roles during our lives—a kindhearted mentor, the soul mate, a trusted friend. Under the best of circumstances, we have the freedom to be all that, but life has a habit of throwing us off course. That means our true callings and most cherished duties get blindsided and wander off to fend for themselves.

To keep going, our aspirations must be made into law—if I accept the responsibility to care, then I must find a way to get it done. As a father, I expect to spend at least one hour each day with my son. One on one, we are doing something together and forging our bond. Am I doing that right now? If not, how can I make this a part of my daily life?

As a spouse, I need to be fully present for my other half, for at least half an hour each day, so that we can maintain our connection, now and into the future. I want to stop, listen, and ask relevant questions, because it will keep us close. Am I doing that right now? If not, how can I make this a part of my daily life?

As a friend, I want to catch up at least once a month and have a proper conversation without judging. Am I doing that right now? If not, how can I make this a part of my daily life?

EXERCISE: YOUR PERSONAL COMMITMENTS

If you want to keep yourself on track with the commitments you make, these prompts might help you get them out of your head.

The first commitment I set out for myself this year is:

....

This is how I'll know I'm getting it done:

....

THE THIRD CIRCLE OF HOPE: SHARING HOPE

The second commitment I set out for myself this year is:

....

This is how I'll know I'm getting it done:

....

The third commitment I set out for myself this year is:

....

This is how I'll know I'm getting it done:

....

When you accept responsibility for people you care about, it gives them hope that they too, can change.

Chapter 14

PATH TO CHANGE

Most people didn't believe in the virus, not at first. "It will burn out before it ever gets to us," they said. But it kept going, like a bushfire, until you could no longer look away.

Like an addict, I kept sneaking out for a hit of the daily news. Record numbers of infections. More lives swept away. Politicians point fingers at each other. The scientists are stumped. Vaccine could be years away.

Standing in the garden, I felt nauseous, and the clouds above me were spinning faster and faster. I leaned against the wall for balance. My chest got heavy—was it the nerves or the virus? I couldn't stay here forever. Tense and hollow, I went back inside.

On the day the restrictions kicked in, I drove out to the reservoir, a reclaimed bushland that still bears the scars of humanity. There was no one in sight, only the trees, shrubs, and the vast body of water that trailed off into the dark sky.

I started running. Up the hill and down again. My legs felt heavy, like lead, but I kept going, reclaiming each step, each turn, as my own. Sweat streamed down my face and into my eyes. I was out in these woods, alone, but with only one thought—forward!

The rain was sudden and hard. It lashed out at me, at my grief and my helplessness. Still, I ran, faster, pushing myself as fast as I could without tripping over the roots and the shattered rocks.

I was free. Free! Free from the death clocks, from stupid thoughts, from the worry that leaked everywhere. The loop was now closed. I came to a stop, panting, and it was enough. From that moment, I knew what I needed to change.

I'm claiming back my life, despite the daze of uncertainty, because this moment, this life, it belongs to me, as my birthright.

THE WHEELS OF CHANGE

It's not easy to get on the good side of change. You have to work for it, or you make the change work for you. It may not be easy, but most change can be tailored to fit you.

There are two wheels of change. One way that change comes about is external. This includes things like the way you are around people, how you respond to the unpredictable, or deal with the obstacles that rise in your way. This wheel of change is constant and unrelenting as you go on through life.

Change can also come from the inside—how you call up the past, the way you make light of a situation, and what leads you to make a decision on the spur of the moment. The wheel never stops moving, try as you might to keep up with it.

In the best conditions, those two wheels of change are aligned. When change arrives from the outside, you have the time to sort through it in your mind so that you can respond to it in a reasonable way. When the change rises up from the inside—a new idea or a worrying thought—you give yourself enough time to act upon it or set it aside.

In either case, there is enough room for you to adjust so that the way that you see yourself is aligned with what you do out in the world.

SURFING ON THE WAVE OF CHANGE

What if you fall on hard luck, and you have not had the time to adjust? What if there is a worry that is eating away at you? Whether the trouble has come from the outside or from within, you may not have had the chance to process it and get back into your usual rhythm.

The two wheels of change get out of sync, taking you off course. You need to bring them back in line to stay on track and wait for the right moment to get back up, like a surfer catching the wave.

Most of the time you spend on the surf goes to reconnaissance. Is this a good wave, or should I let this one go? If it feels right, you get on and ride the wave. Sometimes the luck doesn't go your way, and you are thrown off the board. Then you get up and try again.

Watching the waves won't only allow you to preserve energy, but it will also help you make studied, level-headed choices that might save you from disappointment. The same holds true when you try to keep afloat in the stormy waters of daily life—the key is to stop yourself from rushing in.

I call that *pausing*—taking away the impulse to act.

EXERCISE: PAUSING

Examine the case first, then decide.

Ask yourself:

Does this thought or situation deserve my time and attention?

....

Does it serve me today, or does it serve the future that I want to be a part of?

....

If this is a situation or a thought you can do without, then you can let it go past and keep going.

Then, when the right opportunity comes up, be it a new idea or a situation that can make your life better, you can weigh it up, plan it, and embrace it as part of your day-to-day life.

Staying on track for the life you want is never easy, and many situations you find yourself in are primed to throw you off course.

Take your work inbox—you are sorting through the tasks you want to get done, when you get an urgent email from your workmate. They need help, right now. Urgent! So you drop what you were doing, and you tackle their problem. Before you have the chance to figure out where you left off, a reminder pops up, and you are off into a meeting. Before you know it, half of your day is gone, and you feel like you haven't even begun!

If you can master disruption, you free up the headspace you need to stay on top of uncertainty. This is the mental muscle you flex to weigh up any given situation and decide—is this as urgent as it claims to be? Does this situation deserve my full and undivided attention? Can I put it away to the side and come back to it later?

STEP BY STEP

Pausing can help you deflect negative feelings and divert difficult people away from sapping your time and energy. When you filter out unwanted thoughts and commitments, you free up the mental space to reflect and recharge. This gives you more clarity about what you want to do next and more energy for the people, passions, and projects you truly care about. Pausing will free up the time you need to reach your goals and fulfil your ambitions.

As you take the first tentative steps towards your goal, little by little, you will start to see results. They might not be the final results you were hoping for, but it's enough for you to know that you are on the right track. Those steps build up momentum that keeps pulling you forward. You get an idea and you give it a shot. That shot opens up a new understanding and sets off a chain reaction that keeps you on the path towards the ambition you set out for yourself. The wheels of change begin to turn in the direction you want to go in.

Holding the first printed copy of my book *Simplify Cancer: Man's Guide to Navigating the Everyday Reality of Cancer*, I realised I had the mission to get this book into the hands of every man with cancer. But how? I needed to grow my skills on video, become a world-class speaker and coach, and partner up with others to reach more people. Each idea sprouted a myriad possibilities, and every step beyond the familiar took on a brilliant life of its own. It was the hope that I could be at my best which opened the door, and from then on, I could only try to catch up.

With any new beginning, whether you want to change your career, move house, or start a family, the spark you have on the inside has to adjust the world around you to match. Give yourself enough time to examine the thoughts and experiences that come into your life, and put aside that which you can do without. That way, you'll be able to throw yourself at your true goals, your ambitions, and life's simple pleasures. When the two wheels of change run in line, you are best placed to make the impact you want and help others do the same.

Chapter 15

LEADING WITH HOPE

Nothing is more certain than this—in today's challenging times, we need leaders to guide us through uncertainty, towards hope. If you give courage, guidance, and support to those around you who are struggling the most, then that leader is you, even if you hadn't thought of it that way until now.

You might not give yourself the credit you deserve for the way you lead right now—in your marriage, in your work, with your kids, in your community, and with who you are as a person, as you constantly strive to improve yourself in everything that you do.

The joys you have reached, the sorrows you have overcome, and the frustrations you have learned to live with have given you a unique perspective on life.

You have a distinct take on the way life should be, a vision for what works and what doesn't, and it's vital for you to share your perspective with the people who look to you for help to get through their struggle.

HOW TO LEAD

Accepting responsibility is never easy, be it for the essentials of life or the seminal trends in our culture. Sticking your neck out for a cause that seems out of reach may seem daunting, but taking on a responsibility does not force you to live up to somebody else's expectations.

It is but a chance to dream big and prove to yourself that what you believe in is real. This puts you on the path to making your dreams come to life. Anything is possible, and when you believe that to be true, you will try things no one else will and let your imagination be the guide.

How do you find the inspiration when you are already starved for time? And how can you make room for your goals and ambitions when your plate is already full?

To free up your life, you want to change the way you respond to the situation you find yourself in. When you take away the impulse to act, you can decide what ideas and actions you want to take on, and which thoughts and situations you want to set aside.

In doing so, you get the energy you need to go after your goals. This energy creates the momentum that pulls you forward, towards the bigger ambitions you have in life. The small, incremental changes you make create a ripple effect where one shift triggers another, leading you to be the person you want to be and get the results you want.

In nature, transformation is a necessity, not a choice. The butterfly breaks out of its cocoon because it is the only way it can fly. That's how it works for us too—when you reach the transformation point, there is no going back, and the results are inevitable.

THE FOUR ATTRIBUTES OF LEADERSHIP

So how do you share your vision for hope with the people you want to lead? There are four key attributes people look to for hope in a leader.

The number-one quality we all look for is **honesty**. It's the truth you can't turn away from—you skip past the posturing, and there is no need to be on your guard or read between the lines. Honesty can help you connect with people because they believe in you and your message.

The second attribute of a true leader is having an **open mind**. When you are willing to consider new ideas, people feel safe with you. They can express their worries and concerns. They want to share their ideas, and they are ready to welcome yours. It helps to spark a connection and make peace with our own imperfections.

The third quality people look for is **passion**. We have had enough of empty slogans and slick, polished lines. You want to get behind that guy or girl who is lit up and has a thirst and intensity that you can't deny—it's raw, it's decisive, and you instantly know where you stand.

Being bold is bound to drive some people away—and that's a good thing, because those people were never going to stand by you anyway. And yet, there will be many more people with whom your message will resonate on a deep, personal level.

They will be drawn to you, like a magnet, by the way you hold up your beliefs and the hope you have for the future. Your passion speaks not only to their values, but also to the desire they have in expressing themselves with more freedom and energy than ever before.

The fourth attribute that is vital for hope is **being engaged**. The person you want by your side is the one who isn't going for a small part, but a lead role. They won't stand there and watch—they are willing to dig in, get involved, and make things happen!

They will be present in the marriage. They will be active with the kids. They will help the team. When you listen, when you ask questions, when you share your ideas, you are giving a clear indication that you are reliable and won't back away.

These are the four essential ingredients you need for empathy. When you apply them consistently, using the steps below, they can help you forge stronger bonds with people you care about and have the greater impact that you want in the world.

HOW TO APPLY LEADERSHIP

Step 1—Listen when you want to be heard
Do you remember a time when you sat down with your partner or a friend, and they were completely absorbed in the conversation, hanging on to your every word? They asked deep, thoughtful questions, and the words flowed, like the river. You never felt rushed, and there was nowhere you'd rather be, as if you were enjoying the cool shade on a hot summer's day.

It got through for me when an old friend came to visit me at the hospital during chemo. The world was crumbling all around me, and she came to be by my side and listen. It was such a relief to be heard, and nothing else mattered. There was no need to put on a brave face because I wasn't judged on my performance, and I could speak my mind freely.

And it felt right, to be myself, to be honest and direct, without any drama or show, to bask in full and undivided attention, and to drive the worry away from the inside.

When was the last time this happened to you? For many of us, a conversation like this is a luxury that does not happen often enough. Often, it's the opposite—you run across someone for whom listening is waiting for you to stop talking so that they can barge in with their own agenda.

It is only when you feel truly heard and appreciated that you come alive. When you are recognised for your authentic, true self, any doubt or hesitation falls away, and now, you are ready to listen back.

For your message to carry, people need to feel that you care. Before they put their trust in you and your ideas, people want to be heard. If you want to get their attention, you have to give them your attention first.

EXERCISE: LISTENING LIKE A LEADER

To understand where people are coming from, ask yourself:

Why does this person feel excluded, or misunderstood?

....

What are they missing in their life, and why?

....

We are so immersed in our own world that we forget to tune in with others, and any chance of the connection we might have can slip away without notice.

We need to figure out how we can get rid of the pent-up frustration and worry because if there is no escape route, these worries will keep eating away at us. And what better way to do that then by speaking it out of ourselves—we let our fears out into the open where they have nothing to do with us anymore.

As you listen, you are helping other people release their tension and worry, and by doing so, you become the person they trust and respect.

Step 2—Look out for insight

Having gone back to work after treatment, I ran into an old mate who asked me about my stay in the hospital and the road to recovery. I tried to steer clear of painful topics, but clearly I didn't do a good job of it, since he said, "I am sorry you had to go through this on your own."

There was no pity in his voice, only compassion and understanding. I saw my experience in a new light, my own struggle made obvious, and somehow, it felt more valid.

When you are consumed by the situation you are in, you are often missing a critical insight, some way to make sense of what is going on around you. Explaining the situation in your own words can reveal a new angle or help you to explain someone else's experience.

This is like being in a theatre—what you see up on stage is the exact same show everyone else is watching. The key parts are there for all to see—the story, the set, the actors, and the message. However, looking back on it, you pick out the detail that no one noticed or describe it in a way that no one else would.

Your insight does not need to be complex or refined. A single observation that is thoughtful and well-intended can open a new way of looking at the situation, and help someone make sense of where they are, where they want to be, and how to get there.

EXERCISE: GAINING INSIGHT

When you listen to what someone is telling you, ask yourself:

Yes, but what does that really mean?

....

What are they really trying to say?

....

Is there an underlying message they want to get across, but may not be able to put into words just yet?

....

We don't need to uncover that which is hidden, only to point out what is already there, the essence of what matters to them the most, and why.

Step 3—Lead with questions
Some say they don't like to talk about themselves, but maybe it's because nobody has bothered to ask. It's in our nature to share something of ourselves with others, to

come together, and to connect with other people. You want to open up and you want to give more, when they invite you in and make you feel at home.

When you allow yourself to be curious and focus on the thoughts and feelings of another, you will take time to listen and get lost in their world. You are compelled to go deeper because you want to know more. Immersed in the story, you can't help but ask—so what did you do? What happened next? Did it help?

EXERCISE: ASKING THE RIGHT QUESTIONS

To forge a better connection, ask yourself:

What is this person holding back that they would like to get off their chest?

....

What are they secretly excited about that they have never had the chance to bring up and share?

....

You can never get enough of everyone's favourite topic—themselves. You start where they are and follow the trail. One answer can open the door to another question, and you end up in wonderful places that you could never have imagined.

Step 4—Set your gratitude free

The first time I got hired to speak at a corporate event, I stayed back to talk to the guests. A lady with a kind smile came over and said, "Thank you for what you do in the world!"

I was taken aback, not only by her sincerity and the emotion, but also by how I got swept up in the act of simple and honest appreciation. It struck me how rarely we acknowledge one another, from the impact we have through our work to the trivial details of daily life.

Since then, I have made it my mission to expressly thank the guests on my podcast *Simplify Cancer*, and at the end of every episode, I say, "Thank you for what you do in the world!" And I mean every word of it—I have been blessed to host the most incredible people on my show.

My guests are experts in oncology and wellbeing who share practical advice on living well after cancer, and cancer survivors who talk about their experience to inspire and instruct others to lead happier, more fulfilled lives after cancer. They are my people, and I love being around them. I want to share my gratitude on behalf of myself, and those who love what they do but have never had the chance to express it!

All too often, we go through life without the support and encouragement we deserve. Those around you may have a high opinion of you, but it may never occur to them to put it into words. Yet day after day, you strive to be at your best, and you deserve to have true supporters by your side, cheering you on.

You don't want to point at people's faults—"This is what you did wrong, and this is where you failed; look, you are simply not good at this." You know where that leads—friendships that grow apart, marriages doomed to fail, and bonds that crumble and wither away.

Instead, point out the virtues. Embrace them when they give it their best, cherish the times when they step out of their comfort zone, celebrate every win, no matter how small, and your people will stand behind you and your message.

The advice we give can only be considered sincere when the other person has asked for it and has explicitly singled you out for your opinion. Without the ask, our words of support can come across snobbish or condescending.

THE WORLD NEEDS YOUR LEADERSHIP

It is never easy to sit down and listen. It takes effort to read between the lines and watch out for subtle details. To be grateful for the simplest of things and to choose the right words that will cheer people on.

You need patience to lead—not as a figurehead, but as a trusted guide that others look to for inspiration and hope. A leader that never looks down on people, but brings them up instead, lifting them out of the ordinary and into a higher place.

The world needs your vision of hope, the values you stand for, and the future you want to realise. Now is the time to share your hope for things to get better, to give this hope to your partner, your colleague, your child, your friend, a stranger who may be struggling to find any kind of ledge to hang on to. Your hope can speak to their frustrations, their fears, their private concerns, the dreams they secretly harbor, and the ambitions that may have been put on hold.

The hope that you share is a feeling. Let's say you find yourself lost in a foreign place, and you approach a stranger to ask for directions. They take the time to stop and listen. They are friendly and kind, and it's no trouble for them to show you the way. When they are gone, you are left with a warm feeling that something has gone right in the world today. You feel good because someone was kind enough to show you the way.

This is what good leaders do—they guide you towards the place you were looking to get to anyway. A true leader looks to the future with hope and wants to share that feeling with those who need it the most right now.

Chapter 16

SHARING YOUR HOPE FOR A BETTER FUTURE

It was a wet, cold night in Tamworth, New South Wales, and I had been given the privilege of speaking in the town's library from a thousand kilometres away. Of all the changes the pandemic has brought on, this is the one that I'm grateful for—our new-found ability to teleport across vast distances despite the restrictions. In body, I could not be more than 5 km away from our house, but despite the border closures, I could do a talk half a continent away!

There were four of us on the call: Audrey, Tom, Sarah, and me. I shared the story about the friends that went missing on me during my treatment and how that changed me.

"It made me realise how distant we'd grown over the years... But it turned out to be a blessing in disguise—they kindly stepped aside to make room for people who genuinely care about me." I looked at the faces of my compatriots on camera and asked, "Has something like this ever happened to you?"

After a little while, Sarah spoke up, "Yes, at one point I realised that I was living for somebody else, and never for me. I changed a lot of things about myself, and many of my friends and family didn't like it. But I'm happier now, more than I've ever been."

"Good on you, Sarah, I love the sound of that!", I chimed in. "And what about you, Tom? What's your take on all this?"

Tom smiled, "Well, you're right in that we go through different times in our lives, and that we need to be belong. And so a year ago, I had to get out of Sydney. There were too many hurtful things, so I packed my bags and came here. And now I can talk about it," he said, with a chuckle.

"Love it, Tom!" I exclaimed. "Good on you; that was one bold move you made there, and I'm glad it worked out. What about you, Audrey?"

Audrey looked up in thought and went on to share, "I used to think that breaking off friendships was a bad decision on my part, but actually, I was spot on. Looking back, I don't regret a single thing." Our conversation flowed on, and for me, it brought together the essence of the third circle of hope—sharing your hope with others in a way that lifts you up, to a place of contribution.

Sharing my story through speaking engagements and books has allowed me to share my vision for hope. Stories are how we connect, and when I describe the time I found out I had cancer, you don't think of me in the urologist's office, but of the time you got bad news that you did not want to hear. When I talk about coming home from the hospital, you don't think of me on the swing bench, but of the time in your life when things, inexplicably, changed.

The way you share your story, be it at a job interview, with a friend, or as I often do, in a speech or a workshop, says a lot about you because it's filtered down through your values—the point is not what has taken place, but how you make sense of it afterwards. That is your character, the first station of the third circle, Share Hope.

THE THIRD CIRCLE OF HOPE: SHARING HOPE

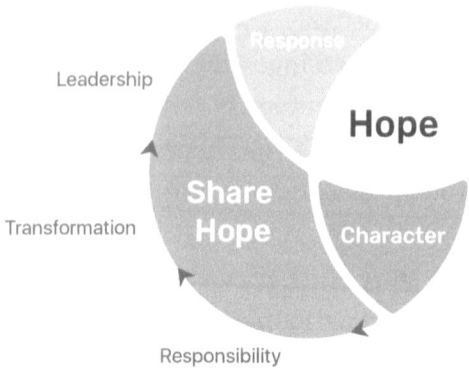

When you share your true, authentic voice, without holding back, then you lead a life that is free of doubt and regret. I know that through writing, speaking, and coaching, I can help people to reconnect with their struggle and find a way forward, but what keeps me going is the commitment I have made to make a difference. It's my calling, just like you have yours, even if you have not had the chance to bring it out into the open. This is responsibility, the second station on the Share Hope circle. The more responsibility you take, the easier it is to give hope to others that they too can change.

But the road is never easy, and I struggle at times to reconcile where I am now and where I see myself in the future. To bridge the gap, I have to get better at working change. This is transformation, the third station of Sharing Hope. When I can stop and evaluate the situations I find myself in to make better decisions about what's right for me, when I stop acting from fear, I know that the wheels of change are carrying me in the right direction.

The last station of Sharing Hope is leadership. To lead, I don't need fancy words or titles, but to remain humble, listen, and acknowledge the struggle that people come up against. I know I won't be able to help every single person, and I might not change their lives in a significant way. But I am okay with that because I know that the times when you go easy on yourself, when you forgive your spouse, when you start to wonder what the future might hold, those moments can hold you together and give you that extra push to stay up and keep going.

You live, and so you lead. It is alone that we suffer, and together... Together, we hope!

CONCLUSION

I grew up in Lviv, on the outskirts of the crumbling empire that was the Soviet Union. It withered out of existence, forcing its many tributaries to fend for themselves. Like the vast majority of its former citizens, we were forced to pick for scraps of what was left. We had to queue for hours each day in the hope of landing a loaf of stale bread against the backdrop of civil unrest.

If you could find the exit, you went straight for it. So that's what my family did, in a hurry. I was thirteen when we left Ukraine for Australia. Imagine Belka and Strelka attempting to settle on the moon—it was survival of the misfittest.

My first foray into the world of endless possibility was simple—the supermarket. I walked around, in a daze, my mind refusing to take in the sky-high abundance. Was this something for everyone or for rich people only? And why were there so many drumsticks—where had the rest of the chicken gone?

I stopped by the dairy section. My eyes moved slowly from one pack of cheese to another. Round, square, blue, grated, with holes... There was no end to it. My head was spinning at the profound injustice of it all, a rift in the universe—*why do some people have aisles of cheese, while others have no cheese at all?*

I want a world where there is enough of the good things for all of us. Enough kindness, enough goodwill, enough to get by, and enough to be happy. But it's up to me, up to all of us, to make it a better place for ourselves first, so that we can then give this feeling of plenty, this hope to those who are still waiting to catch a break.

There is no denying that we are at different stages of our lives, and these stages are not abstract, freestanding monuments, but they are intertwined to reflect our experience in all their supreme guts and glory.

First, there is the struggle. That is where the first circle of hope begins, in a place of hardship, where you might be fighting hard just to stay afloat. Just like you, I have lived through the struggle, and while the circumstances that each of us face might be unique, there is still a lot that we have in common. It is in those times of struggle that you feel scared, and you can't stop thinking about all the things that could go wrong. You have no idea what's going to happen next.

So you start looking for answers, since that is the only way. For a while, it may be hard to believe that things could change, but the first step to hope is accepting that the struggle is here and soaking in the magnitude of the situation you find yourself in, because it opens up the door for what you might do next. For it is only when you walk into a dead end that you realise there must be another way out.

There is usually no easy way, so in the first circle of hope, you want to figure out what's going on and decide what you should do next. The best way to do that is to take your worries and likely outcomes out of your head. Write them down on paper, where you can see exactly what they stand for so that you can make decisions that are not driven by emotion, but by good sense and sound judgement.

And when emotions do take over and fear sweeps in, it might be easier to get out of the way. Find a quiet place where you can be on your own and breathe. Steady yourself to weather the storm without trying to control your emotions or prevent yourself feeling a certain way. Trying to prevent certain feelings is exhausting, and in my experience, it only makes things worse! Let those worries play out because that is all they are. These are the rolling waves of raw emotion, so let them sweep in and ride past, leaving you be.

There will be times when you feel alone, and it feels like no one gets you and nothing will ever change. It's a tough place to be, but those walls don't have to hold you! You are not alone, my friend, and it's the right time to accept your place in the world and accept that you are one of us. Turn towards those around you for hope, to those who care and want to be there for you without getting in the way. This cuts right to the core of Finding Hope, the first circle of hope, where you look to lean on your community, your family, your friends, your workmates, experts and other people who can be your true supporters in a difficult time.

If you find it hard to accept help in the first place, then it might be easier for you to start by *giving* help. Helping those who need it the most paints this experience in a different light because you can see the difference it makes in a real, tangible way. You will know what to expect, and it can make you feel like you have earned the right to get help in return.

Another stage of life is when you start dreaming of reaching new peaks and fulfilling your ambitions. This is when the second circle of hope, Build Hope, comes into play.

Conclusion

Isn't it true that when you make bold moves in life, it is crucial to deal with the inevitable obstacles that rise in your way?

It's easy to give up when you lose your hunger to keep going, when you get thrown off course by problems you did not expect. That is the precise moment when you have to get in touch with your life purpose. You can find the exact wavelength on which your sense of purpose resides, for when the call of your purpose is strong, you are much more likely to stay on track.

You might have many competing tasks on the go as you are chasing your big dream, and it can be hard to wait for it to turn true. That is why it is important to celebrate every win you have along the way, every little step that is edging you closer because you can feel that your dream is alive, and it's real, and it's out there, within your reach.

When you bring up those moments when you start winning, when you give them a name and make a note of them in your diary, each and every day of your journey, they give you confidence, spurring you on, to the point where action becomes an afterthought because you are compelled to move forward, towards the life you want.

The confidence you build will serve to charge your resilience, to keep going when things don't go your way and life pegs you back a notch. You know it's coming, and that is why you build your resilience by expecting challenges and bringing yourself up to face them on your terms. Resilience rounds off Building Hope, the second circle of hope, as you make your way towards fulfilling your ambition.

And then, you might find yourself in yet another stage of your life where you have survived the immediate struggle, and you have gathered enough hope to be in a position where you want to share it with others. No one checks your credentials on the way in—you give when you are ready to give. With this, you are riding the third circle of hope.

Sharing Hope is giving the hope you have for the future to the people around you. You can bring out hope in someone who may be struggling right now. You don't do it because it's the right thing to do, but because it's ingrained in you, it's how you are wired. This is the first station of Sharing Hope.

That station is your character, because it can be hard to have a greater impact without immersing yourself in your personal values. You develop a more profound understanding of who you are as a person and what you stand for, and in a way, you acknowledge that it doesn't matter how you are judged by others because it's not about you anymore. When you want to lead, when you want to guide and inspire others, you aspire to make a difference to a cause that is bigger than you or anybody else.

Your character is reflected in your values, which lead you to responsibility, the second station of our circle of sharing hope. I cannot look at the world and expect to leave it in the same state I found it in. I have hope that the world will be a safe, more just place for all, and I take full responsibility for that.

I cannot take credit for most of the good things that could happen, but I accept that I must do my part in order to make a small difference. In order to make a change, I have to change the way I manage my thoughts and the situations I find myself in.

Instead of reacting in a way that might not serve me or what I want to do in the world, I want to spend more time qualifying my thoughts, my emotions, and the way I interact with the world to see if it fits. Only then I can fulfil my purpose and share the hope I have with others.

That is the hallmark of leadership, to be the change that you believe in. No worrying and no looking back. For why worry about all the things that could go wrong, when there is so much we can make right?

OUTRO: ACCEPTING HAPPINESS

To break up the road trip, we stopped in a little town near the mountains. The place was so small it barely made it onto the map. We arrived at dusk, with kangaroos coming out to greet us at the front porch of the holiday house we had booked.

There was only one pub in town, and it was already closed. "You know, I could eat everything," my son cried out. I left the family to unpack and drove out to the next town for food and supplies. Before long, the fuel gauge arrow hit zero, so the drive was sluggish and tense. I breathed a sigh of relief when I finally pulled up at the petrol station.

In the supermarket, I found spaghetti, tuna, and ketchup, before I got back on the road, flashing the car's headlights into the night. Back in the house, we left our improvised meal unfinished—where had the hunger gone? The

Monopoly game had no dice, so we flicked through the pile of old magazines and random books on the coffee table and made our way to bed.

The night kept leaking strange sounds into our lonely house, and with the broken lock out the front, we could only hope nothing or nobody would find its way inside.

In the morning, the sun sneaked up on us, flooding the bed—come and meet me outside! I brewed a strong pot of coffee, found the only cup with a handle, and put my feet up on the front porch.

The world around me stood still, timeless and deliberate. I saw a mountain peak piercing the sky out in the distance. The air was pure and infinite, like the road. The worries and discomfort had disappeared, and I smiled, because they had made it all worth it.

This holiday came and went like any other—not as one pure, unbroken state of bliss, but in a zigzag: short bursts of tranquillity and joy, punctuated by worry and the mundane.

IDENTIFYING HAPPINESS

Just as our happy snaps can dull out the arguments and plans gone astray, so we must measure our happiness in sporadic moments of ecstasy. When you weave those fragments of joy into the fabric of everyday life, you become happier, as you notice how they make you feel over time, and this feeling becomes the norm.

But these moments are easy to miss, like an old friend you might walk past in the crowd. We tend to drift towards the epic achievements that are few and far between, and it's easy to rush past happy memories or forget they were there in the first place.

Happiness is not a flat line, but a patchwork of a-ha moments, tiny little wins that make you feel alive, and pivotal moments when you almost gave up, but somehow, found the strength to get up and keep going.

RECOGNISING MOMENTS OF JOY

When you look closely, you will recognise those moments at once. The joy fragments are waiting for us to pick them out and hold them up as a sacred part of our experience.

They are the things that help you calm your mind and soothe your soul—potting around in the garden, holding your lover's hand, enjoying a quiet moment alone with your thoughts. They come together and flow, like music.

Give them a life in your diary to reflect on what makes you happy. This simple daily ritual can help you celebrate the little things that went your way and give you a sense of progress, on your terms.

Morning is the perfect time to look back on what you achieved the day before because it sets you up for the day ahead, and you expect more good things to come your way.

EXERCISE: FINDING JOY

Here are three prompts that can help you bring those joy fragments to light:

When I think of a moment yesterday when I felt genuinely happy, what is the first memory that comes to mind?

....

When I think of a moment yesterday when I was content, what is the first moment that comes to mind?

....

When I think of a moment when something felt right yesterday, what is the experience that comes to mind?

....

Outro: Accepting Happiness

We don't always achieve life-changing breakthroughs in our daily life, but we are all striving to be at our best. Every chore you get out of the way, every task you get over the line is an accomplishment on your part, and you should treat it as such!

This is no time to be modest or doubt what you do in the world—trust yourself, because after everything you have been through, you are enough! Enough to stay alive, enough to be loved, enough to go for your dreams, enough to lead, and more than enough to be happy. We cannot create happiness out of nothing, only accept what is already here and recognise that it's hidden in plain sight.

It is crucial for us to realise that we sometimes are the only thing standing in the way of our happiness. Even when we have the very best intentions, it is easy to slip into negative habits and thoughts. In other words, it is not only helpful to focus on things that make us happy, but also to identify how we sometimes self-sabotage in order to prevent it from happening.

EXERCISE: PREVENTING NEGATIVE FEELINGS

You don't need a to-do list, but this shortcut will help you get as far as you possibly can from trouble, pressure, and outside demands. Use these prompts in combination with your diary:

What is the one annoying thing that I can refrain from doing today?

....

What is the one good deed I can do today, without expecting anything in return?

....

No one ought to be turned away from happiness—there is enough for you, me, and the rest of us, now and forever more.

Today, you deserve happiness, and it's here for you, waiting for you to accept it with open arms!

GET IN TOUCH

For practical ideas and inspiration for living a happier, more fulfilled life, sign up for my weekly email newsletter at PowerToBeHappy.com.

Are you looking for a speaker for your next event? Or would you like to work with me one on one for support in taking the next step in your life?

Email me at joe@simplifycancer.com today.

ACKNOWLEDGEMENTS

I did not plan to write this book. It came to me when the pandemic started. It's been a revelation, but I could never have done it alone... Thank you for being a part of it and helping me on this quest!

To Olya, for giving me courage and keeping me sane. To Mike, for your art and the crazy good times. To Max, for the sunshine.

To my family. To my grandma, for showing me what matters most. To my grandpa, for being the dad. To Leo Babiichouk, the doppelganger. To my mum, for her unconditional love.

To my friends—thank you for sticking through with me! To Troy Walters, for believing in me and supporting me in everything I do—it means so much to me. To Igor Asmaryan, you are the selfless hero—I can't thank you enough! To Kevin Flattery, Oleg Pogreb, Denis and Ev Semchenko, for the good times. To Lee Kelemen, for having my back.

I am fortunate to have found the most incredible people through *Simplify Cancer*. To Khevin Barnes—you brought the book title to life and will always be my soul twin! To Lee Silverstein, for bringing out the best in me and the world. To Rita Corrente and Jared Toh, for making a world of difference. To Suzanne Chambers, for the inspiration. To Jim Adams, there is a river of hope running through you! To Darryl Mitteldorf, you rock. To Dave Pook, for believing in me. To Lucy Byers, for what you do, now and into the future. To Helen Santamaria, for the trust. To Daniel Sencier, because you listen. To all the incredible guests on the podcast, your stories and life-changing work are making this world a better place!

I discovered many things about myself, and the world, at the University. Thank you for the experience! To Jill Mancarella, thank you for speaking the truth! To Mark Williams, the voice of reason. To Kay Darbyshire, for watching my back. To Alicia Fayle and Nicole Robertson, for the optimism in spite of everything.

In a strange way, the restrictions due to this virus made me realise how much freedom I enjoy and how proud I am to be living in Melbourne. We have an amazing

Acknowledgements

community here in Frankston! I can't thank you enough. To Thomas Moore, for aiming high and fighting for excellence. To Megan Hough and Mark Longley, for your friendship. To Ross Macdonald, for running in the same direction. To the Frankston Toastmasters family for making me a part of a greater whole.

Thank you to Peter Doherty for leading the charge.

To the doctors and nurses who have saved me, my wife, and our sons so many times. Thank you!

www.ingramcontent.com/pod-product-compliance
Lightning Source LLC
Chambersburg PA
CBHW020323010526
44107CB00054B/1959